Christmas
Prayers

Dearest Ellen,
    May your life be
filled with the blessing
of good health, and an
abundance of love, joy
and peace! Love,
            Sherfae

Christmas
Prayers

A Heartwarming Collection
of Holiday Blessings

PAUL M. MILLER

BARBOUR
PUBLISHING

© 2013 by Barbour Publishing, Inc.

Print ISBN 978-1-62416-221-3

eBook Editions:
Adobe Digital Edition (.epub) 978-1-62416-481-1
Kindle and MobiPocket Edition (.prc) 978-1-62416-480-4

All scripture quotations are taken from the King James Version of the Bible.

Cover image: ImageZoo Illustration/veer.com

Published by Barbour Publishing, Inc., P.O. Box 719, Uhrichsville, Ohio 44683
www.barbourbooks.com

Our mission is to publish and distribute inspirational products offering exceptional value and biblical encouragement to the masses.

Member of the
Evangelical Christian
Publishers Association

Printed in the United States of America.

Contents

Introduction

So, how do you expect anyone to find time to say Christmas prayers? Me and mine barely have time to shop the family gift list, thaw a turkey, get the spare bedroom ready for Auntie, and decorate the house (not in that order). My rushed prayer is usually nothing more than "Dear Lord, help us not have a total meltdown before December 24th. Amen (whew!)."

If this reflects your frame of mind when anticipating the most glorious days of the year, these prayers, or conversations with God, are for you. They are really thought starters, directed to turn your mind toward the heart of your heavenly Father.

Prayers are personal. No third party can ever express what's on your heart or write in your unique lingo or dialect, but when it seems the whole world is attempting to make this holy Advent and Christmastide one huge commercial, with very little spiritual content, don't join in— talk to your heavenly Father about it.

Find a semi-quiet spot, push aside the sale ads and menu planning, and allow yourself to revel in the beauty, the bliss, and the blessings of this sacred season.

PAUL M. MILLER

The Beauty of the Season

Ever since that surprising night in Bethlehem, more than two thousand years ago, artists, wordsmiths, and musicians of all persuasions have attempted to express the beauty of the Christ event that has captured the hearts and imaginations of the whole world.

It has been said that beauty is in the eye of the beholder. Perhaps this is true, but because of Christmas, those who behold and believe can also experience beauty in their hearts and souls.

THE NATIVITY

The birth of Jesus Christ was on this wise. . . .
That it might be fulfilled which was spoken
of the Lord by the prophet.
MATTHEW 1:18, 22

*H*eavenly Father, we know the story so well; we've read and sung about it a thousand times. Our children even put on bathrobes and act it out—the birth of Jesus. The event is printed on our calendars in bright red letters, and for believers it's inscribed in our hearts as a personal Christmas special!

But the cast You selected for this first nativity drama were not actors, but ordinary folks. Assure me that the commoners, like the sheep wranglers and the overwrought innkeepers—ordinary people like me—were as necessary to Your salvation scenario as the road-weary carpenter and his fragile pregnant wife, Mary.

Father, throughout my preparation and celebration of this Christmas season, give me reminders that its beauty is more than a perfectly decorated tree; it's in a manger and Your love. Amen.

THE NATIVITY

*Mary was espoused to Joseph, before they came together,
she was found with child of the Holy Ghost.*
MATTHEW 1:18

*L*ord, in this season of beautiful music and words, decorated houses and wide-eyed kids, I need to pause and reread the sacred text. I want to be sure that I know what's really at the heart of Christmas.

The nativity story has become so commonplace that many people have it committed to memory. Consequently, I might be tempted to gloss over the too-familiar words, to the neglect of what You want to teach me. I pray that the words "she was found with child of the Holy Ghost" be as important as "peace on earth."

It is right for Mary's husband, Joseph, to be praised for his care of the child Jesus, but I never want to forget that You, Father God, are the baby's true Father. Maybe the innkeeper and the shepherds didn't fully understand the plan You were setting in motion, but please remind me that Jesus is Your Son and that my faith is founded on the knowledge that You are also my Father. Amen.

THE NATIVITY

Joseph her husband, being a just man, and not willing to make her a public example. . .took unto him his wife.
MATTHEW 1:19, 24

Faithful God, another facet of Christmas is certainly reflected in Joseph's trust in Mary. I thank You that real love has a way of igniting trust.

While Joseph is often depicted in art as a gray-haired old man, and his beloved Mary as a mature woman with a halo, I know that Mary was a teenager, and Joseph perhaps a young village man, who probably had hopes and dreams of a carpentry shop and a bright future.

I'm sure the angel's news of Mary's pregnancy was a shocker, but Joseph loved and trusted her, as You trusted him.

Lord, I want to live my life above suspicion and distrust. Teach me to live and love in such a way that those around me will recognize You in me. Amen.

THE NATIVITY

The book of the generation of Jesus Christ,
the son of David, the son of Abraham.
MATTHEW 1:1

*H*eavenly Father, if there's one thing everyone has plenty of, it's Christmas photos. Most of them are classic poses that are generally the same from year to year. And then there are the really precious ones that find their way in or onto our Christmas cards and annual family letters.

But at the time of Jesus' birth, family history was recorded in words, not images. Matthew's Gospel calls Jesus' history a "book of the generations." Still, we who are so used to all the intimate details of TV interviews, have but Mary's response to the angelic messenger and her song (Luke 1:38, 46–56) as a record of her inmost thoughts about motherhood and her child, the Savior.

Father God, impress deeply in my mind and heart Mary's prayer, "Be it unto me, according to thy word." May I echo those words in my own life. Amen.

THE NATIVITY

She shall bring forth a Son,
and thou shalt call his name JESUS.
MATTHEW 1:21

*L*ord, I'm so glad that You know me by name. A lot of families have traditions about the naming of a child, and it was no different with Bible families. There was a time when special relatives were honored by giving the newborn his or her name. But today it's become more of a private decision between the parents-to-be.

Whatever the traditions in Mary's and Joseph's families, they were certainly shattered by the intervention of Your heavenly messenger. There would be no Joseph Jr.; You named Him Jesus.

Dear Lord, thank You for being interested in me. I'm in awe that I can be on a first-name basis with the God of the universe. I'm not sure if I'll ever see an angel, but during this Christmastide, I pray that we'll draw even closer. Actually, that I will draw closer to You. You are already here with me. Amen.

THE NATIVITY

He shall save his people from their sins.
MATTHEW 1:21

Father in heaven, Jesus' sacrifice may be too serious a topic for this time of year, when everything is poinsettia red and Christmas-tree green. Why, in the great plan of heaven, did it take the birth of a boy in a troubled, far-distant land to make forgiveness and new life possible? Animal sacrifices upheld Your law for hundreds of years—but I praise You for offering us a better way through grace—Jesus.

At first glance the sacrifice of Your Son can seem un-reasonable to a twenty-first-century person. I admit, so much of the "why" of Christmas appears to have been lost in holiday tissue paper. And perhaps this is a Good Friday reflection, but I want to soak up the great depth of Your love for me in sending Jesus, the final sacrifice, so that I could be forgiven.

As I celebrate the joy of a long-ago newborn child, help me to remember that He is also Messiah, my Savior. Amen.

THE NATIVITY

All this was done, that it might be fulfilled which
was spoken of the Lord by the prophet.
MATTHEW 1:22

*G*od, it seems that parents always ask their newlywed children something like, "Well, when do you plan to start a family?" which in turn causes great embarrassment or uproarious laughter.

According to Matthew, the birth of Jesus had been anticipated and foretold by Hebrew prophets for as long as anyone could remember. It was one of Your promises that was going to happen "in the fullness of time." That is, according to Your godly calendar. Every Jewish mother probably held an unspoken wish that her baby would be the Messiah.

Thank You, Lord, for Your provision for my salvation. . . that I have been in Your mind and on Your heart since the beginning of time. Amen.

THE NATIVITY

They shall call his name Emmanuel,
which being interpreted is, God with us.
MATTHEW 1:23

Father, names were of utmost importance to people in Bible times. Today many newborns are named after popular movie stars and entertainers. The significance of names seems to have disappeared.

But the name *Emmanuel* was Your promise to Your people—Your long-expected Son.

Father, the name Emmanuel is so in keeping with Your deep love for me, for us, for Your whole creation. "God with us" is the age-old promise that You would be here on earth with us—that You would walk with us again and break the barrier of sin that was erected between You and Your creation in the garden of Eden.

Thank You for Your presence in my life. Help me to keep Emmanuel as part of my Christmas celebration. Amen.

THE NATIVITY

Her firstborn son. . .JESUS.

MATTHEW 1:25

*L*ord, it's often obvious who the firstborn child in the family is. When it's a boy, his parents may honor his father or grandfather by christening him with that relative's name. And sometimes with a title.

On the first Christmas the boy in His manger cradle was given a most common name—Jesus or Joshua, which means "Salvation is in God." Lots of kids playing in the Nazareth dust had the same name. Our Lord bore a commoner's name.

I sometimes forget that in Your heavenly wisdom, Jesus was raised in a family. He had brothers, also with common names like Joseph, Simon, James, and Judas. He went to synagogue school and worked with his brothers and dad in a carpenter shop.

When I light the Christmas candles this year, I want to remember Jesus as a man among men, and at the same time, the Light of the world—my Savior. Amen.

THE JOY

Good tidings. . .
LUKE 2:10

*H*eavenly Father, the shepherds' reaction to the angel's good news was fear and probably bewilderment—more curiosity than joy. I'm sure they didn't immediately catch the implications of "a Savior." It wasn't until they saw the child that joy set in. They saw Him, they heard Him, and He touched them. All at once the meaning of a Savior became personal. The result was joy—amazing joy—shareable joy—that they spread to their rustic world.

I'm sure too many of us still equate Christmas joy with our childhood excitement; when it was all wrapped up in a Santa-stuffed stocking and lots of presents. Or maybe our joy comes from seeing the children "have a good Christmas."

Dear Lord, make me a shepherd this year. Remind me to reveal a Christ-reflected joy that is a greater gift than the best present in the whole world. Amen.

THE JOY

My spirit hath rejoiced in God my Saviour.
LUKE 1:47

God, how refreshing to read that Mary rejoiced in the angel's news that her baby was to be the Savior of the world—news that opened a spigot of happiness and exceeding great joy within her teenage heart.

Even in her youth, Mary understood that what she was about to experience was from You. No doubt friends and family who didn't understand questioned the news. If Mary lived today, her Nazareth neighbors might have tried to shame her into aborting the child within her. Instead, Mary rejoiced in the angel's announcement.

My Lord, the knowledge of Your will was upon Mary and gave her the courage to rejoice in her situation. Thank You for those who revere life. Let believers work with You to give our society loving concern for the unborn. Amen.

THE JOY

There were in the same country shepherds. . . .

LUKE 2:8

*L*ord, it's difficult to think of any less joy-producing job than taking care of sheep. Yet sheep have importance in Your story. Jesus is called both "the Lamb of God" and the "Good Shepherd." You also call us sheep when we go astray. Sheep were sacrificial offerings, and in parables they were superior to goats.

Because sheep have such a prominent position in scripture, it isn't any wonder that You sent their keepers, the Bethlehem shepherds, a direct heavenly announcement of Jesus' birth. Tradition says the shepherds brought a lamb to the Christ Child and laid it in the manger with Him and explained, "This is all we have."

Father, what better gift is there than "all I have"? In this season of gift giving, help me to remember to give back to You. Amen.

THE JOY

Behold, I bring you good tidings of great joy.
LUKE 2:10

*H*eavenly Father, good news is always welcome at Christmas. Yes, the chore of sending cards can become overwhelming, but when they are in my mailbox—they become "good tidings."

Sometimes the annual Christmas letter is a chore to read as well as to compose. I hope and pray that Christmas tidings never stop being a reason for joy! Remind me throughout the year to pray for those who send me cards each Christmas.

Unfortunately, not all tidings are joyful. During these years of world conflict and crazed behavior, sorrow is no respecter of season. Father, I pray for those families that are facing change and struggle. May the angelic message of peace on earth lend a note of hope where there is no earthly comfort.

Let me be a giver as well as receiver of glad tidings in the spirit of Jesus. Amen.

THE JOY

Fear not.

LUKE 2:10

*L*ord, few things can suck the joy out of life like fear. Real or imagined, the enemy of my soul realizes that when I'm "sore afraid," all joy is swallowed by that fear.

One of Your assurances of Christmas was delivered in dramatic fashion to sleeping farmhands in the dead of night. The deliverer was a heralding angel with a startling message—the birth of a Savior—but the shepherds weren't ready to hear it, they were smitten with fear.

"Don't be fearful," the angel prefaced his good news. "There is reason for joy!"

Father, Your assuring hand is a stabilizing influence for Your children. Fear or dread should not be an attribute of the believer. John the apostle of love assures us that "perfect love casteth out fear" (1 John 4:18). My reason for joy is the good news of Jesus. Thank You for casting out my fear, so I can live in Your joy. Amen.

THE JOY

Let us. . .see this thing which is come to pass,
which the Lord hath made known unto us.

LUKE 2:15

*F*ather, my heart and mind are still with those shepherds on the night shift. It isn't fair to sell them short. Tending sheep hadn't dulled their intelligence. After they recovered from their angelic encounter, they were certainly aware that You were behind the extravagant announcement, and in all probability, what awaited them in Bethlehem.

Lord, I want to be able to recognize You behind the issues of my life. I don't believe in coincidence; I believe that You are involved in my life and continue to make known Your will for me. I want to have the assurance that You are at work in my life.

Use the events and spirit of Christmas to teach me and touch others. I want to make Jesus known. That's the source of authentic Yuletide joy. Amen.

THE JOY

They came with haste and found Mary, and Joseph,
and the Babe lying in a manger.
LUKE 2:16

*F*ather in heaven, I cherish the joyful anticipation that accompanies the Christmas season: the mouth-watering smell of turkey, the all-out excitement of children opening their gifts, a visit with a long-time-no-see best friend.

Usually I believe that good things are worth waiting for, but how time can drag when I'm waiting for something that brings me joy. It's no wonder that the shepherds were spurred on with haste and excitement by what awaited them in Bethlehem—a baby that would make all the difference to the world.

Lord, thank You for the gift of Your Son. In my own anticipation of presents and good food and time spent with family, keep the joyful expectation of the shepherds as they visited the Savior in my mind. Amen.

THE JOY

*When they had seen [Jesus] they made known abroad
the saying. . .concerning this child.*
LUKE 2:17

*L*ord, sometimes I miss opportunities to tell other people what You've done for me—and the whole world. The story of Jesus' birth reminds me that the shepherds were so excited by the coming of Your Son that they couldn't wait to run home and tell everyone.

Father, I want to be filled up with so much joy at Your love for me that it spills over onto everyone around me. Whatever happened to the shepherds in that Bethlehem stable gave them the get-up-and-go to tell everyone back home what they had seen and heard. I can just hear their enthusiastic retelling of the heavenly announcement: "Can you believe it? Angels talking to Amos and me?"

What transpired in that stable must have had a great impact. A mother, a dad, and in a manger, a tiny newborn baby. Whatever was revealed that night to common shepherds gave them the motivation to share the news that they had seen Your Son.

That's what I want—the fearless desire to talk about Jesus. Amen.

THE JOY

Mary kept all these things,
and pondered them in her heart.
LUKE 2:19

*G*od, it's not hard to imagine that after their long journey, a search for housing, the birth of her Son, Jesus, and a visit by a clan of rambunctious shepherds, that Mary needed some quiet time.

Luke's Gospel draws a curtain of privacy around the young mother in her attempt to prayerfully consider and make sense of all that had transpired in her life—Luke says she *pondered*.

Pondering Your wonders and workings takes nothing away from my joy. Like Mary, I often find my mind swimming with Christmas details—with life details. The needs and responsibility of family, as well as day-by-day worldly pressures take their toll. That's when You, Lord, encourage me to step into some quiet time and ponder the wonders of Your involvement in my life.

Lord, help me to step back from the hectic chaos of life this Christmas and dwell on the joy that comes from You. Amen.

THE SONGS

Suddenly there was with the angel a multitude of the
heavenly host praising God, and [singing].

LUKE 2:13

*H*eavenly Father, I know Your inspired account of Jesus' birth reports that the heavenly host *spoke* their "Glory to God," but something in me wants to *sing* those beautiful words about peace and goodwill for earthlings like me.

Thank You for the inspiration of Christmas songs and carols—how a baby's birth brought joy to the world and made a silent night holy.

Father, You gave us bright-eyed little kids to beautifully sing about Your child. Who can ever forget a preschool choir's parent-pleasing rendition of "Away in a Manger"? Particularly those simple words of the last stanza: "Be near me Lord Jesus; I ask Thee to stay close by me forever and love me I pray."

Thanks, too, for those moments throughout the rest of the year when I need to be reminded that "God imparts to human hearts, the blessings of His heav'n." Amen.

THE SONGS

Sing unto the LORD. . . .
For great is the Holy One of Israel.
ISAIAH 12:5–6

God, one of the most wonderful joys of Christmas comes from the songs of the season: caroling, singing in church, or listening to others "proclaim Messiah's birth." Singing to You is a cherished form of praise at Christmas.

Lord, I'm grateful for the hushed atmosphere of worship on Christmas Eve: a candle-lit sanctuary, an organ accompanied by a guitar or piano. I can feel Your presence as the setting and familiar words of scripture and lyrics prompt me to remember Christmases past, and the people who were part of them.

Is it any wonder that through long centuries godly people have used songs for worship, as well as to express joy and sorrow? You told us to sing a new song to You (Psalm 96:1). You are our strength and song (Isaiah 12:2) and the One who gives us a song in the night (Job 35:10). Lord, this year I pray that You will fill my heart with a new song for You. Amen.

THE SONGS

Let all the angels of God worship Him.

Hebrews 1:6

*H*eavenly Father, angels and Christmas go hand in hand—from a Bethlehem hilltop to the top of a Christmas tree.

> *Angels from the realms of glory,*
> *Wing your flight o'er all the earth;*
> *Ye who sang creation's story*
> *Now proclaim Messiah's birth.*
> *Come and worship, come and worship,*
> *Worship Christ, the newborn King.*
>
> James Montgomery

What would any Sunday school pageant be without little girls vying to play the angel's role? While little girls may look better in wings and tinsel halos, Father, I worship You this Christmas just as the angels did so long ago.

Lord, I may not be acquainted with guardian angels, but still, I thank You for their involvement in Your plan. Amen.

*Bethlehem. . .out of thee shall he come
forth unto me. . .to be ruler in Israel.*

Micah 5:2

*L*ord in heaven, a favorite verse of the familiar Bethlehem hymn is sometimes skipped (it can get cold caroling):

*How silently, how silently the won-
drous Gift is giv'n;
So God imparts to human hearts the
blessings of His Heav'n.
No ear may hear His coming: but in
this world of sin,
Where meek souls will receive Him
still, the dear Christ enters in.*

Phillips Brooks

Father, the phrase, "meek souls" is often a stumbling block to many souls who'd like to sing this verse, but *meek* doesn't have to be an off-putting word. No one objects to "Blessed are the meek" (Matthew 5:5), because of Your promise that they will inherit the earth. I know that *meek* describes the one who submits to Your will, just as Jesus submitted His life on earth to Your will—even to the point of death. Father, give me an extra helping of humility. "Not my will, but thine, be done." Amen.

THE SONGS

Make a joyful noise all the earth. . . . For he cometh.
PSALM 98:4, 9

*H*eavenly Father, some may call it noise, but at Christmas I call it singing—joyful singing!

> *Joy to the world! The Lord is come;*
> *Let earth receive her King;*
> *Let every heart prepare Him room,*
> *And heav'n and nature sing.*
>
> ISAAC WATTS

How did You inspire Mr. Watts to write "Heaven and nature sing"? It's as if he heard the shepherds, celestial chorus, combined with the sweet sounds of the natural world: the majestic harmony of a soft wind in pine branches against the sharp staccato of raindrops and a tympani-like roll of thunder. All together they provide a royal welcome to the King of kings and Lord of lords.

With or without any vocal or instrumental abilities, we are invited to prepare You room in our hearts: "Come in today, come in to stay, Lord Jesus." Amen.

THE SONGS

He hath sent me to bind up the brokenhearted,
to proclaim liberty to the captives.

ISAIAH 61:1

*L*ord, living on this side of the first Christmas, it is difficult to totally understand the tragic physical and spiritual needs of Your chosen people, as well as their neighbors. This Advent hymn for a yearning people in bondage sums up how they must have felt:

> *Come Thou long expected Jesus,*
> *Born to set Thy people free;*
> *From our fears and sins release us,*
> *Let us find our rest in Thee.*

CHARLES WESLEY

Father, what was true of bound people in Isaiah's vision and Charles Wesley's hymn, also resonates with our contemporary world. Isaiah's forecast of a God-King who would bind up and make free those under the strong arm of wicked political and satanic power was met with indifference, until Your Son was born, an answer for "every yearning heart." Lord, I'm so thankful that You have set this captive free. Amen.

THE SONGS

That holy thing which shall be born of thee
shall be called the Son of God.

Luke 1:35

Heavenly Father, there are few Christmas hymns with the power of "O Holy Night." Granted, much of its appeal centers on the classic musical setting by French composer Adolphe Adam. But the third stanza really speaks to our day:

Truly He taught us to love one another;
His law is love and His gospel is peace.
Chains he shall break, for the slave is our brother.
And in His name all oppression shall cease.
Sweet hymns of joy in grateful chorus raise we,
Let all within us Praise His Holy name!
Christ is the Lord! O praise His name forever!

John S. Dwight, translator

As millions sing these promising lyrics in Christmas sanctuaries around the world, dear Lord, may the words change the hearts of all who repeat them. Amen.

THE SONGS

Comfort ye, comfort ye my people, saith your God.
ISAIAH 40:1

God, Your inspired, majestic prophet Isaiah proclaimed some of the most reassuring and soul-searching words to be found in all of the Old Testament. His promise of comfort was and is held tightly to our hearts today. An anonymous English composer caught a vision of the prophet's message:

> *God rest ye merry, gentlemen;*
> *Let nothing you dismay,*
> *Remember Christ our Saviour*
> *Was born on Christmas Day*
> *To save us all from Satan's power*
> *When we were gone astray,*
> *O tidings of comfort and joy, comfort and joy!*
> ENGLISH CAROL

It probably goes without saying that a hymn writer's inspiration is not on the same par as an Old Testament prophet's, but some early English Christian "gentleman" expressed the reason for Jesus' birth, ministry, and death in no uncertain terms. I pray that all the merry men and women under my roof may understand the peace and rest we have in You. Amen.

THE SONGS

He came unto His own.
JOHN 1:11

*H*eavenly Father, the thought of Jesus coming to His own is mind-boggling. He left His glory in heaven to come and live among a wretched people. Charles Wesley's "Hark! The Herald Angels Sing" speaks of Your plan for Jesus:

> *Hail, the heaven-born Prince of Peace!*
> *Hail the Sun of Righteousness!*
> *Light and life to all He brings,*
> *Ris'n with healing in His wings.*
> *Mild He lays His glory by,*
> *Born that man no more may die,*
> *Born to raise the sons of earth,*
> *Born to give them second birth.*
>
> CHARLES WESLEY

He came to be one of us—the sons of earth! To give us light and life and healing. He laid aside His glory to give us eternal life through a second birth. Thank You, Father. Amen.

THE SAVIOR

Fear not: for, behold,
I bring you good tidings of great joy. . . .
Unto you is born this day. . .a Saviour.
LUKE 2:10–11

*L*ord, there's that word again—*Savior*, with a capital *S*. I've seen the word used to describe a first-responder who saves lives, but the capital *S* is reserved solely for Your Son, Jesus.

I often wonder if a stranger looking in on the family from Nazareth, with Jesus asleep in a feeding trough, could even suspect He was the Wonderful Counselor, Everlasting Father, Prince of Peace (even the Mighty God!) whose coming they'd prayed for? That child in a manger was the Savior of the world, who saves us from our sins.

Artists have painted a golden halo over Jesus to show He was Your Son, the Savior. Today I am fully aware of my salvation—the Savior lives within my heart. Dear Lord, I just want You to know that my need of a Savior is always with me. Amen.

THE SAVIOR

This is indeed the Christ, the Saviour of the world.
JOHN 4:42

*H*eavenly Father, I like the image of Jesus' "Saviorhood" that is relayed in John's Gospel. It speaks to me in very personal ways. In a Broadway play titled, *Family Portrait*, Mary tells John, "Even on the night He was born, I knew He was special." And John responds, "He said He was the Savior of the world." An audience member advised the playwright, "He did know He was the world's Savior, and so did every man, woman, and child who came in contact with Him."

God, I know that the Christmas story cannot remain in that Bethlehem stable. Jesus lived a purpose-driven life. The sweet child in the manger had a mission, and Mary was intimately aware of that calling—Your angel had told her.

I want to learn from Jesus' purpose-driven life. Give me courage and direction to share the message of my Savior. Amen.

THE SAVIOR

I am the way, the truth, and the life:
no man cometh unto the Father, but by me.
JOHN 14:6

*H*eavenly Father, neither Matthew nor Luke provide any details about the reactions of visitors to the Bethlehem stable on the night of Jesus' birth. It would have been enlightening if there had been a reporter on hand to record initial reactions to the baby.

In my imagination, besides shepherds, others stopped by the cattle shed that night. Perhaps someone who had lost his way popped in for directions; or the innkeeper checked to see if everything was okay. No doubt their reactions to the child would have been the same: "Handsome boy," "My, He has strong lungs," "What do you think He'll be when He grows up?"

That last remark is the easiest one to answer: "He's going to be the Savior of the world." And to the one who needs direction, "He will be the Way!"

Lord, may He be the truth and life to those who celebrate His birth this Christmas. Amen.

THE SAVIOR

The Father sent the Son to be the Saviour of the world.

1 JOHN 4:14

God, when we're pushing our overflowing shopping carts down an aisle at the neighborhood grocery store, accompanied by the ever-present music to shop by, often we recognize a Christmas carol melody and whisper-sing to the familiar tune: "Chri–ist the Sa–vior is bo–orn, Chri–ist the Sa–vior is born." But then we turn and read the nutritional contents on the back of a box.

Father God, do You ever get annoyed by our casual attitudes about Your Son? Or does it please You that at least we sing along with a song about Jesus? If I were You, I'd probably answer yes to both.

Lord, please forgive my indifference to Your sacrifice. At times I get distracted by life. Show me when I should shout out to the whole wild world, "God's gift to us is His Son, Jesus—the Savior!" Amen.

THE SAVIOR

God sent. . .his Son into the world. . .that the world
through him might be saved.
JOHN 3:17

*H*eavenly Father, many brave men and women deserve huge, heartfelt thank-yous for their bravery and caring. We're grateful for the life-saving abilities of those who respond to accidents, disasters, or violence. But, Lord, while they may be able to save our physical bodies from harm, only You can save our souls and give us eternal life with You.

I am so glad that I met You, my Savior. The only Christmas gift that I need this year is the gift of Your Son, who came into this world to die for me.

Thank You, God, that my name was on the gift tag attached to my gift of salvation. Amen.

THE SAVIOR

Ye are not your own. . . . Ye are bought with a price.
1 CORINTHIANS 6:19–20

God, hopefully it isn't common for average people to momentarily forget who they are. But if I'm stopped by a traffic cop after a day of Christmas shopping, I may even forget my name before finding my all-important driver's license hiding behind some overused credit cards.

While forgetting *who* I am is a little embarrassing, it should cause real concern to forget *whose* I am. As a believer in Christ I know that I am not my own; I know it's Jesus who has saved me, not my personal charm or clever abilities, but Your Son.

In the spirit of Christmas, dear Lord, I want to inform all who enter my home that the little baby in the manger scene is more than just festive decor, He represents my Savior, the One who paid my price. Amen.

THE SAVIOR

I am the door: by me if any man enter in,
he shall be saved.
JOHN 10:9

*H*eavenly Father, it's difficult to understand why some friends and family turn their backs on Jesus and His gift of eternal life, especially at this time of year. All around us are decorative reminders of what Christmas is all about, often symbols of our Lord and Savior.

Front doors often announce the reason for the season. The traditional evergreen wreath with a sprig of red holly (real or not) reminds friends and family that the circular shape of the wreath represents eternity and Your forever-and-ever quality; the evergreen foliage bespeaks eternal life; the holly's color is a graphic reminder of the cross.

Father, I pray that Christmas visitors will discover more than a decorative front door. May they be introduced to the One who declares, "I am the door"—Your Son, our Savior. Amen.

THE SAVIOR

There is none other name under heaven given among men, whereby we must be saved.

Acts 4:12

*L*ord, Shakespeare wrote, "What's in a name? A rose by any other name would smell as sweet." In a celebration of Jesus' birth, Juliet's question can be answered, "In the name of Jesus, who bears the name, the Rose of Sharon, we have a Savior."

An ancient Christmas hymn calls Your Son "the Christmas Rose." The anonymous poet continues, "He blooms to tell all His world that the sweet fragrance of salvation emanates from Him." Rather flowery language for the truth of which Luke wrote; it's only in His name can be found salvation.

Lord, may my life emanate the very essence of Jesus' work within me. Amen.

THE SAVIOR

To the only wise God our Saviour, be glory and majesty,
dominion and power, both now and ever.

JUDE 25

Father God, the poet Phillips Brooks's holiday lines, "Everywhere, everywhere, Christmas tonight. . .O sons of the morning, rejoice at the sight" wonderfully describe the Christmas spirit that permeates the air—it's on the street, in homes and shops, featured in TV commercials, and on the mind of every child of any age.

Lord, sometimes I get caught up in the excitement and forget the "who" behind the annual holiday parade, the tree lighting, the animated holiday window displays, and the so-called winter holiday school vacation.

While the book of Jude has no direct references to the birth of the Christmas "who," it does speak to the "why" of this season—Jesus as Savior, endowed with "glory and majesty, dominion and power." Though probably not realizing it, for such a One my friends and neighbors have sought all their lives.

Father, please give me the insight to find ways of sharing the truth of my Savior. Amen.

The Busyness of the Season

For reasons known only to the inspired Gospel writer Luke, the birth-of-Christ narrative is populated with busy folks. With a little imagination, it reads like the *Directory of Overextended Regular People in and Around Bethlehem*. It isn't impossible to imagine the shepherds telling the angel, "Just a minute please, I'm trying to get this lamb cared for." Or an innkeeper's wife in the kitchen hollering, "Will somebody get the door, I'm up to my elbows in dirty dishes?"

The message of Christmas has to cut through all our busyness or it is a holiday and not a holy day. Like any overextended community, the City of David was humming with activity. But like the lowly shepherds of Bethlehem, we must put aside our planning and baking and shopping and acknowledge the reason for the celebration—the Messiah has come.

THINGS TO DO

There went out a decree from Caesar Augustus that all
the world should be taxed. . . . And all went to be taxed,
every one into his own city.

LUKE 2:1, 3

*H*eavenly Father, last year I prayed, "*Help!* My got-to-do list is longer than a child's letter to Santa Claus, and I'm running out of time." It isn't much better this year.

I can certainly identify with the pressure Mary must have faced when Joseph came home from the carpenter shop and told her of their impending trip to Bethlehem. Why can't my celebration of Your Son's birth somewhat reflect the simplicity of the actual happening? Why should I complicate the most encouraging event in history because of what the world decrees it to be?

Father, please add my name to Your to-do list; give me the will and understanding to create a Christmas season that gives me time and energy to celebrate Jesus Christ. Amen.

THINGS TO DO

And all they that heard it wondered at those things which
were told them by the shepherds.

LUKE 2:18

*L*ord, I'm wondering if my enthusiasm for Christ is observable by people who encounter me at the store or around town. Folks seldom ask, "So, why are you so upbeat this morning?" If they did, I'd probably say, "Must be the latte I just had," when in fact, I had a good prayer time, or I heard something great on Christian radio.

Conversely, folks who ran into the shepherds after their intro to Jesus must have asked, "Hey, what's up with you guys? How come all the rejoicing and stuff?" The men could have responded with some good news about the sheep, but they didn't! They talked about Jesus.

God, while I'm running my holiday errands let my love for You and my joy in Your sacrifice overflow onto everyone I meet. Remind me to ask myself, "Does this person know why Christmas means so much to me?" Lord, give me enthusiasm to tell them. Amen.

THINGS TO DO

When eight days were accomplished. . .
his name was called JESUS.
LUKE 2:21

*F*ather God, after the birth of any child, the average family is in a state of recovery. In the case of the Bethlehem birth, eight days after Jesus' arrival it was necessary for the family to assume its responsibility to fulfill the laws of their faith. It was the thing to do.

No cartoon character of the expectant dad, Joseph was the responsible man You knew him to be. Bundling up his little family for the five-mile trek from their stable, he got them on the road to the great temple in Jerusalem. Their task? To honor God in the presentation of their Son for circumcision and naming. The rite was performed by a temple priest and overseen by parents and friendly witnesses.

Lord, it is a blessing to imagine Mary's smile when ceremoniously asked, "What is His name?" and in complete obedience she replied, "Jesus." Father, help make obedience the Christmas theme of my life. Amen.

They brought him to Jerusalem. . .to offer a sacrifice.
LUKE 2:22, 24

*H*eavenly Father, it's traditional in some homes to conduct pre-Christmas family meetings in which gift spending and the like are discussed. Fathers point out the need for sensible spending and the need to sacrifice.

But this is the season to be jolly, why the word *sacrifice*? Isn't this the time for excess—overspending and over-eating? Another reading of today's scripture indicates that the Nazareth family's sacrifice was of the temple variety, a ritual for ceremonial cleansing for the new mother. The law required the sacrifice of an unblemished lamb for the rite, but Joseph's financial situation allowed for two turtledoves.

Lord, our extravagance at Christmas doesn't find its genesis in Mary and Joseph's sacrifice. Extravagance is found in Your gift from heaven—Jesus Christ. Because of Him, the sacrifice has been made. Thank You. Amen.

THINGS TO DO

When eight days were accomplished for the circumcising
of the child, his name was called JESUS.

LUKE 2:21

*L*ord, Jesus' name is a vital part of the Savior's story.
Here, it is connected to His circumcision, the must-do rite
for every Jewish boy eight days after his birth. The time
when He officially receives His name.

I sometimes forget Jesus' Old Testament *Jewishness.*
His childhood was influenced by a strict adherence to the
Torah or Law, the first five books of the Bible, where salvation could be found only in the keeping of thousands of
rules and regulations.

But, Father, You knew differently. So did His mother.
He was to be called *Jesus,* because He'd save His people
from their sins.

How correctly penned the hymn writer: "The King of
Kings salvation brings, the Babe, the Son of Mary." Amen.

[Simeon] came by the Spirit into the temple. . .
took [Jesus] up in his arms. . .and said. . .
"Mine eyes have seen thy salvation."
Luke 2:27–30

*F*ather, sometimes every one of us needs confirmation that our choices and decisions are correct. It's always helpful when someone at the Christmas dinner table says, "I really like your pie, may I have the recipe?" Reassuring, too, is the gift receiver who says, "Just what I wanted!"

Is it unbiblical to believe that Mary and Simeon's experience in the temple was a verification that both needed?

Though he heard no angel voices or shepherd report, Simeon knew salvation had arrived when the Nazareth family entered the temple court. And Mary must have experienced the thrill of confirmation from the old man's praise.

The folks who people my world deserve such a confirmation, too. Is it too far-fetched to believe that it's possible for a contemporary Simeon to see Jesus because of me? Lord, help me point the way to You this Christmas. Amen.

THINGS TO DO

And there was one Anna. . .[who] served God with
fastings and prayers night and day.

LUKE 2:36–37

*H*eavenly Father, no doubt most of us know more about serving kids and the boss at work than we do about serving You.

The post-Christmas story continues in the temple with the introduction of an elderly woman named Anna. No sooner had the family bade good-bye to Simeon than they came face-to-face with the eighty-four-year-old widow who worked a twenty-four-hour shift in the temple. Her job was fasting and praying—that was her service.

Lord, help me remember that *fasting* doesn't have to be an uncomfortable word; when coupled with prayer, as it most often appears in scripture, it's a means of service that brings Your purposes to life.

Father, I want to increase my prayer service, show me how to make time in all my busyness. Help me see that serving the kids or a boss can also be service for You. Amen.

THINGS TO DO

*When they had performed all things according to the law
of the Lord, they returned. . .to their own city Nazareth.*

LUKE 2:39

*G*od, after the hustle and bustle of Bethlehem and
Jerusalem, it was time for Mary and Joseph to saddle the
donkey, bundle up the baby, and set out on their trip home
to Nazareth.

It would have been interesting to have heard their
conversations en route. Mary possibly was compiling a
honey-do list, though a cradle and chest of drawers may
have already been in place, Joseph being a carpenter. And
there must have been excited conversation over introducing
Jesus to His grandparents and the rest of the family.

More revealing may have been Mary's unspoken
thoughts. The concerns of a woman who realized she was
the mother of the world's Messiah.

Even at Christmas, Father, we all have gnawing
thoughts about family. Teach me to trust You more. Give
me more of Anna's prayer life and Mary's obedience. Amen.

THINGS TO DO

And the child grew, and waxed strong in spirit. . .
and the grace of God was upon him.

LUKE 2:40

*H*eavenly Father, I wonder if there were times when Mary momentarily forgot her Son's deity, and looked at Him as a kid who was growing too fast. Did she ever comment to Joseph, "It just seems like yesterday that we bought Him those sandals, and they're already too small."

Like any boy of His time and place, Joseph taught Him a trade. As other boys were born into the family, there were probably the usual brotherly squabbles and noise. And like any mother with a few minutes alone with her own thoughts, Mary may have slowly reexamined those things that she had pondered in her heart.

Father, You know that all of us at one time or another have heart-pondering secrets or situations that we must face in our lives. In too many families the annual Christmas get-together becomes a time to dig them up or criticize one another. Lord, may one of my "to-dos" be to let Your grace move among us. Amen.

PLACES TO BE

And Joseph also went up from Galilee,
out of the city of Nazareth. . .unto the city of David,
which is called Bethlehem.

LUKE 2:4

*L*ord, it isn't unusual this time of year to feel the pressure of places to be and people to see!

For lots of us, one of the distinct pleasures of Christmas is experiencing family. For some, that means travel; those of us who have to take Yuletide trips to kith and kin sometimes dread those few days' drive with a backseat full of kids asking, "Are we there yet?" But it's Christmas!

Father, it's really hard to imagine how pregnant Mary and concerned Joseph made their eighty-mile, one-week journey from Nazareth to Bethlehem on donkey back, but then, isn't it what awaits us at the journey's end that really counts?

Lord, when I'm with family or friends at home or out of town, I pray that I'll reflect the reason for the gifts and good times—the journey—Jesus. Amen.

PLACES TO BE

Now when Jesus was born in Bethlehem of Judea in the
days of Herod the King, behold, there came wise men
from the east to Jerusalem.

MATTHEW 2:1

*H*eavenly Father, those august men we call wise
men, or kings, or magi perfectly illustrate the "place to be"
of Christmas. For them, it was kneeling and worshipping
the King of the Jews.

Matthew's description of those mysterious men is not
conclusive, neither are we sure how many men there actually were, or even where they found their newborn King.
Nonetheless, they calculated their route, gathered up gifts,
saddled their camels, and took off toward a star pointing to
the place where He was, and they were to be.

Father, launching out into the unknown is frightening.
Too often the sky is dark, without a single star in sight—a
good time to hum, "Guide us to Thy perfect light." For I
know that You are my Guide. Amen.

PLACES TO BE

There came wise men. . .saying,
Where is he that is born King of the Jews?
MATTHEW 2:1

*G*od, the meeting between the magi and King Herod is just one more example of Your involvement in our Savior's birth. Such a confrontation had to have been part of a Master plan. In fact, the whole nativity story is a major drama that was scripted to bring to pass the plan of salvation. In many ways the magi were in the wrong place at the right time. They were committed to find a King, but they were in the wrong court.

Lord, are You really aware of me down here? When I pray, "deliver us from evil," do You understand that "us" includes me? Please keep me from wandering into the wrong court. I thank You for Your direction—for the directional "stars" You put in my life. Amen.

PLACES TO BE

We have seen his star in the east,
and are come to worship him.
MATTHEW 2:2

Heavenly Father, Christmas worship has a special beauty. It can take place in a stable, as per the shepherds; in a church, where many of us will gather Christmas Eve; or in a "house," where the wise men find Jesus later in the narrative.

What constitutes worship? The Bible extols its practice and necessity, but doesn't provide a how-to blueprint for its practice. The atmosphere and surroundings are secondary to our desire to stand or kneel in awe of You. Worship, too, is a deep longing for more of You in our daily lives. It's to participate in praise of You with friends and loved ones.

John Byrom of the seventeenth century advised that each man should approach You "in manner and ways that best suit him." And that all You require "is trueness of heart, and love for Jesus Christ." Lord, this Christmas I want to express my love for You in worship. Amen.

PLACES TO BE

Herod the king. . .was troubled. . . . He demanded
of them where Christ should be born.
MATTHEW 2:3–4

*L*ord, why is there so much trouble at Christmastime? The news reports are full of it, and people we all know are experiencing it in spades. And now, in the nativity narrative, Jesus is potentially facing it.

It's clear why King Herod was a troubled ruler; all people with nefarious plans should be troubled. The contrast between "Peace on earth, goodwill toward men," and the Herodian plans is troubling.

Unfortunately, folks of peace and goodwill are not exempt from trouble at Christmas. Tragedy and accidents are no respecter of season. Neither is illness, nor the disappointment kindled by the uncaring among us. So how does the believing heart face such crisis? Father, help me remember what was prophesied of Jesus and spoken by an angel: "His name shall be called Emmanuel, which means 'God is with us.'"

"Be near me Lord Jesus; I ask Thee to stay close by me forever and love me I pray." Amen.

[Herod] sent them to Bethlehem, and said, Go and search
diligently for the young child; when ye have found him,
bring me word again, that I may come and worship him.

MATTHEW 2:8

God, a child diligently searched for is often a lost child. Not so Jesus, He was safely tucked away with family, far from harm's way.

Today department store Christmas shopping can be a lost-child trap. A mom's too-long decision making at some uninteresting counter is a sure opportunity for a bored youngster to wander over to a more interesting display, eventually causing a public address system to announce, "Tommy Jones, your mother is waiting for you in the glove department."

Back in the second chapter of Luke's Gospel, when Jesus was twelve years old, His parents discovered they had lost Him in the temple. When found, He expressed His first acknowledgement of who He was: "I must be about my Father's business" (Luke 2:49). This was probably another moment that Mary tucked away in her heart.

Father, I pray that those who are searching for Jesus will truly find Him at Christmas. Amen.

PLACES TO BE

Lo, the star, which they saw in the east, went before them. . .and stood over where the young child was.

MATTHEW 2:9

*H*eavenly Father, how many young men decked out in bathrobes and gold paper crowns have marched down a center church aisle singing, "O star of wonder, star of night, star with royal beauty bright. . . . Westward leading still proceeding, guide us to thy perfect light."

And none the worse for wear they always find their place up on the church platform with a youthful holy family. Their number must be legion.

The journey that the magi undertook is most impressive. Matthew doesn't provide a mileage or time chart, but even the most casual reader can imagine the obstacles those determined men from eastern regions experienced. What drove them westward? A strong desire to find the One, for whom they had sought all their lives.

Without a doubt, they had discovered their place to be. Lord, grant me the diligence to continually seek after You, the willingness to follow You even as far as those wise men did. Amen.

PLACES TO BE

When they were come into the house,
they saw the young child with Mary his mother.
MATTHEW 2:11

*L*ord, one can hardly comprehend what is meant to actually *see* the young child who was Jesus. Artists' interpretations have influenced the modern mind's eye.

The Bible is silent with specifics. No one knows what the eastern travelers expected. They seem to be single-minded in their search to worship the King!

Tradition describes the wise men as learned magi, students of the heavens, eastern religions, and scripture. They were seekers of truth and salvation.

As a result of their studies, each was convinced the King he sought would guide him into greater truth, and the star would lead him to the place where that truth would be found, the cradle of a newborn King.

Into the baby's presence the three men stepped. To their knees they fell. Into their hearts came the realization: "[Our] eyes have seen thy salvation, which thou hast prepared before all people" (Luke 2:30–31). Father, I praise You that the salvation the wise men found is also mine. Amen.

PLACES TO BE

They presented unto him gifts.
MATTHEW 2:11

*H*eavenly Father, of all the people who experienced the baby Jesus—shepherds, innkeepers, temple personnel, and now wise travelers from the East—probably none had greater impact than those men tradition has named Melchior, Balthazar, and Kaspar. Three, who carried gifts: a chest of gold, a flagon of frankincense, and a chalice of myrrh.

Gold, because He was a King. . .frankincense, for the worship of God. . .and myrrh, for burial. These learned men knew the person they sought.

Evidently Christmas gift giving has its roots in this very familiar episode in our Lord's biography. Each present was practical and had a distinct purpose in the child's life and death. But, Father God, our much-loved practice of gift giving is also an acknowledgement of Your gift of our Savior—Your Son, Jesus. Amen.

NEEDS TO MEET

[Joseph was] to be taxed with Mary his espoused wife,
being great with child.
LUKE 2:5

*L*ord, while no one wants to bring up taxes, money is something on many people's minds at Christmas. In the spirit of the season we're supposed to be concentrating on giving—to friends and family, not to the government.

During the Christmas season the air is rich with the chiming of bells as Salvation Army bell ringers shiver beside their red kettles on sidewalks throughout town while a homeless person on the corner holds up a battered cardboard sign wishing passersby a "Merry Xmas."

Sharpen my senses, Father. Give me eyes to see and ears to hear and a heart that is in tune to the needs of humankind. Let my heart be broken as much for those who are spiritually bankrupt as it is for those who have no worldly possessions. In my own life, give me wisdom to deal with the spiritual issues around me as willingly as I drop some coins in those red buckets. Amen.

NEEDS TO MEET

*My God shall supply all your need according
to his riches in glory by Christ Jesus.*
PHILIPPIANS 4:19

God, sometimes I wonder if the apostle Paul was quoting You properly in declaring that You would supply *all* my needs. That's quite an order at Christmastime. It seems like most kids' letters to Santa contain enough requests to bankrupt even heaven's treasury.

But I know Your riches far exceed our human imaginations, and Your promise is in the Bible, so it must be true—to everyone, not just to the church folks at Philippi. Is the word *need* and not *wish list* a clue to the extent of Your generosity?

Christmas is the perfect season to be part of Your riches. Ours are the only hands and feet and pocketbook You have on earth. Lord, my prayer for this day is open my eyes and heart to the needs around me; show me where I can be Your hands, feet, and pocketbook in the name of Jesus. Amen.

NEEDS TO MEET

If ye then, being evil, know how to give good gifts unto
your children, how much more shall your Father which is
in heaven give good things to them that ask him.

MATTHEW 7:11

Heavenly Father, even at Christmas there are difficult days—maybe even a week or month is more accurate. Sometimes I neglect my personal needs when I'm caught up in the busyness of doing for others—family, friends, the church. Sometimes I'm overly occupied with everybody else's wants.

But it is satisfying to make kids happy. Especially at Christmas we all try so hard to give them everything that they desire. Even if we have to shop for hours and wait in long lines to find that one special toy, it's worth it when we see the smiles on their faces on Christmas Day.

But Matthew's emphasis isn't on the kids in our lives, but on Your generosity, God. This verse makes it clear that it is permissible for me to approach You and make some request on my own behalf.

Father, what good thing do You have for me if I ask? It appears that Your only requirement is that it must be good. Thank You for this promise and the reminder of how much You desire to give blessings to Your children. Amen.

NEEDS TO MEET

Let us therefore come boldly unto the throne of grace,
that we may obtain mercy, and find grace to
help in time of need.

HEBREWS 4:16

*H*eavenly Father, boldness is a difficult attribute for a lot of us to assume, especially when it comes to dealing with life issues—like selecting a Christmas tree. Families who prefer live trees know the agony of considering bald spots and poor posture. There's little worse than a humped-over Christmas tree. When artistic merit is a big deal, then boldness is needed in making the right decision, just one more yuletide pressure.

I know that Christmas tree selection seems like a small thing, Lord, but I want to carry the boldness I have when making small choices into the weightier aspects of life. I want to come to You in my time of need knowing that I am already forgiven. Lord, thank You that through Your Son I can boldly come before Your throne. I praise You for offering grace and mercy to one such as I. Amen.

NEEDS TO MEET

Whoso hath this world's good, and seeth his brother have
need, and shutteth up his bowels of compassion from him,
how dwelleth the love of God in him?

1 JOHN 3:17

*L*ord, heaven-inspired Henry Van Dyke created Artaban, a fourth member of the magi, in his story "The Other
Wise Man." Artaban also began the star-led journey to find
the King with three precious gifts: a sapphire, a ruby, and
a pearl. But meeting human need along the route cost him
not only his gifts but also the opportunity to present them
to the child.

His wanderings consumed thirty-three years of his life,
until on a street in Jerusalem he experienced an earthquake,
"the result of a crucifixion on Mt. Golgotha." A heavy stone
pediment shook loose in the quake and fell on Artaban. In
his final moments of life he heard his long-sought King
speak: "In as much as ye did it to the least of these My
brothers, you did it unto Me." At last, the other wise man
met his King.

A fictional story, Lord, but an eternal truth for me.
May I look at every interruption or request this Christmas
as another opportunity to serve You. Amen.

NEEDS TO MEET

Your Father knoweth what things ye have need of,
before ye ask him.

MATTHEW 6:8

God, the subject of need at this time of year sends me back to where Christmas started, on the road to the little town of Bethlehem. In my heart I picture a young husband attempting to make his pregnant wife comfortable on the back of a donkey. The multi-day trek meant camping in fields en route.

I can imagine moments at the nightly campfire where Mary is preparing an evening meal as Joseph cares for the animal. Stretched out on blankets with a canopy of stars overhead, Joseph prays: "Lord, You know what awaits us up ahead. At this moment our needs are many, and we place them all in Your hands."

Father, You must have replied, "I know what things you need. I'm taking care of them. Trust Me." Thank You for providing what I need. Amen.

NEEDS TO MEET

Your heavenly Father knoweth that ye
have need of all these things.
MATTHEW 6:32

*H*eavenly Father, does what You promised Mary and Joseph go for me, too? Or is it reserved for that family? I suspect Your response is "You are family."

It's interesting to note that Matthew records the adult Jesus, in the midst of ministry, assuring His followers that You are fully aware of their needs. It sounds almost self-serving to have these concerns, but for many people, need is not just a Christmas thing—it's a 24/7 situation. It's the need for a job, the need to feed a family, the need to repair the car in the garage. . .the need for a *house,* much less a garage.

Father, help me find comfort in Jesus' assurance that You know all about my problems, but also give me the desire to use my own talents to help others in their times of need.

Please let Your work begin in me. Amen.

Then I commended mirth, because a man hath no better thing under the sun, than to eat, and to drink, and to be merry: for that shall abide with him of his labour the days of his life, which God giveth him under the sun.

ECCLESIASTES 8:15

*L*ord in heaven, it's cookie-baking time again. For most, that means checking the pantry for baking supplies and then a trip to the grocery store for the needed ingredients. Or some of us may be tempted to buy those rolls of cookie dough that you can bake just like the real thing then ice, decorate with red and green sprinkles, and pop into Tupperware with no one the wiser—not even the neighbor who's a cookie-baking whiz.

It's important to celebrate together, and Christmas cookies are an essential part of the holiday season. Kids love the creative activity, even though they make such a mess, their icing and decorating can be so crazy, and they've been known to eat more than they decorate! Father, as I labor to finish all of my Christmas tasks, help me "to eat, and to drink, and to be merry" with those around me. Amen.

NEEDS TO MEET

He which soweth bountifully shall reap also bountifully.
Every man according as he purposeth in his heart,
so let him give; not grudgingly, or of necessity.
2 CORINTHIANS 9:6–7

*F*ather, in a recent survey the three spiritual needs mentioned most often are (1) the development of a generous spirit, (2) a renewal of childlike faith, and (3) sharing spiritual concerns with family and close friends. While sharing personal needs at Christmas may never take the place of carol singing and gift opening, in honest moments most of us admit to having some needs that can only be met by You, Lord.

But often I could help others if I would allow You to use me for Your purposes, Lord. I want to give generously—not just of my money, but of my time and knowledge as well. Sometimes it's too easy to ignore the needs of other people. I get distracted by my own problems and wants, and I become blind to the poverty around me.

Father, in the coming new year nurture in me a more generous spirit. Help me to give willingly and cheerfully. Amen.

A SAVIOR TO SERVE

Be not forgetful to entertain strangers: for thereby some have entertained angels unawares.

HEBREWS 13: 2

*H*eavenly Father, how many of us have actually entertained angels without knowing it? Christmas folk tales are full of such stories. A favorite involved the town cobbler who gave a poor downtrodden traveler a pair of shoes and an invitation to spend the night, only to discover the next morning that, in fact, he had entertained his Savior, Jesus Christ.

Random acts of kindness are most certainly ways of serving the Savior. Offering to pay for the lunch of a not-too-well-off college student might just end in a conversation about You and someone new finding Jesus as their Savior. According to Isaiah, that takes fearlessness and recognizing the presence of God.

Dear Father, give me a greater desire and courage to share Your good things with others. Amen.

A SAVIOR TO SERVE

What doth the LORD require of thee, but to do justly, and
to love mercy, and to walk humbly with thy God?
MICAH 6:8

*H*eavenly Father, this scripture spells out serving the Savior rather succinctly. Some might say, "But that's Old Testament, I'm a New Testament Christian." You respond, "The birth of Jesus does not diminish My pre-Bethlehem expectations for My people."

According to scripture, history, and human experience, justice, mercy, and humility are basic requirement for service. They most certainly reflect Jesus' ministry; consequently, they should become ours.

In the warm glow of Christmas light, let me gather loved ones near and share poetically what serving You requires:

Let every heart keep its Christmas within:
Christ's pity for sorrow, Christ's hatred for sin,
Christ's care for the weakest, Christ's courage for right,
Christ's dread of the darkness, Christ's love of the light,
Everywhere, everywhere, Christmas to-night.

PHILLIPS BROOKS

Amen.

A SAVIOR TO SERVE

*[Mary] brought forth her firstborn son, and wrapped him
in swaddling clothes, and laid him in a manger.*

LUKE 2:7

*L*ord, I often wonder how You respond to our attempts
to reenact the Bethlehem Christmas event. I like to think
that You smile when our kids assume the roles of those
familiar characters.

A young actor begs the innkeeper to give them a
room with such passion that the little girl actress bursts
into tears and rewrites the script with "Oh, come right in,
Joseph, we'll just make room!"

Father, making room for the Savior has been a theme
for as long as we've celebrated Jesus' birth. I believe the real
discussion today should not be "Happy Holidays" versus
"Merry Christmas," but rather "Am I actually serving the
Savior who began life wrapped in swaddling clothes?"

Lord, I want to be more aware of the love bands that
You have wrapped around me, and to swaddle those close
to me with that same love. Amen.

A SAVIOR TO SERVE

*The servant of the Lord must not strive; but be gentle
unto all men, apt to teach, patient.*

2 TIMOTHY 2:24

eavenly Father, this is the season of Christmas cards. Not to mention decision making time: Should they be cute and whimsical or deeply religious with scripture? Do I have to write notes, or can I enclose a form letter? Am I striving?

There is a gospel song called "Give of Your Best to the Master." Lord, what is my best? Right now I'm overwhelmed with Christmas preparation. I'm doing my best to make everybody happy, but at times it feels like "I dare you not to have a Merry Christmas!"

Father, I'm really trying hard to be an acceptable servant. I understand that I'm serving You when I serve others in Your name and spirit—even when I'm doing Christmas cards. Give me more patience, please. Amen.

Put on therefore. . .mercies, kindness, humbleness of
mind, meekness, [and] longsuffering.
COLOSSIANS 3:12

*L*ord, it looks like giving myself to You includes chairing a church committee—again! It seems that often, with all humility and meekness, we try to turn down church positions we don't want, but our longsuffering pastors always seem to compliment us into them: "No one can handle it like you can."

So we end up standing on a ten-foot ladder attempting to coax a stubborn tree-top star to shine with "royal beauty bright" in order to relive the joy and wonder that permeated the sanctuary in the previous year's tree-lighting service. To see on a myriad of faces the reflective glory of a thousand little white lights and a beckoning star. Lord, give me a spirit of kindness and help me to remember that "inasmuch as ye have done it unto one of the least of these. . .ye have done it unto me." Amen.

A SAVIOR TO SERVE

Thou therefore endure hardness,
as a good soldier of Jesus Christ.
2 TIMOTHY 2:3

*G*od, in a letter home at Christmas, an overseas-stationed PFC describes his plans for putting Christ in an infantry Christmas: "We found a bush and decorated it with paper chains like we made in kindergarten. On the top branch we attached a star that I'd cut out of cardboard and wrapped with aluminum foil borrowed from the mess hall. Mac rounded up some birthday candles, which we stuck on with chewing gum, and one of the guys lit with his lighter.

"We sang 'White Christmas,' then I started strumming 'silent night, holy night, all is calm, all is bright,' and someone started singing it with me. This led to a long discussion of Christmas back home, including going to church.

"Mom and Pop, keep praying for me, I want to be serving the Lord, along with serving my country." Lord, show me opportunities to serve You wherever I am. Amen.

I was an hungred, and ye gave me meat: I was thirsty, and ye gave me drink: I was a stranger, and ye took me in.

MATTHEW 25:35

*H*eavenly Father, serving dinner to down-and-outers at a soup kitchen may not be everyone's idea of an appropriate Christmas Day activity. Still, many have found such a ministry can make the day even more meaningful. There's something rewarding about postponing the family dinner for a few hours, donning an apron, and offering a plate of turkey and stuffing to the hungry and thirsty. It's the satisfaction of doing for others, and the thrill of reminding guests You are a Lord of love.

Jesus' parable on hungry and thirsty strangers is spot-on as a lesson in serving. Those who hunger and thirst for a holiday meal may become those who hunger and thirst after righteousness.

I pray that You would lay on my heart a sense of responsibility to serve food and provide hospitality wherever I am, in the spirit of Jesus. Amen.

A SAVIOR TO SERVE

[Be] servants of Christ,
doing the will of God from the heart.
EPHESIANS 6:6

*L*ord, in one of those newspaper advice columns, a questioner asked if giving gifts out of obligation was acceptable to the spirit of Christmas. The columnist replied, "It seems to me in the spirit of the holiday, giving ought to come from the heart."

The heart has been blamed for things romantic ever since a man named Valentine wrote love notes and became a saint. Previously, philosophers believed it to be the control center of one's will, as did the apostle Paul: "Do the will of God from the heart."

Serving Christ is a heart issue—love and will are intertwined. "I want to serve because I love Him."

That's my desire, Lord. I want all that I do for You and for others to come from my heart. When other motivations influence me, check me and remind me of today's scripture. Amen.

A SAVIOR TO SERVE

By love, serve one another.

GALATIANS 5:13

*F*ather God, a Christmas folk story involves a young juggler from a poor village, who prayed nightly to perform his art in a Christmas competition before the king: "He will reward me," the young man told his parents. "Then I will show our villagers how I love them."

Because of the distance, on the day of the contest the boy arrived too late to compete. But the king, reading the boy's heart, asked him to juggle anyway.

Standing before a sculpture of the manger, the little juggler performed with grace and dexterity. While the crowd wildly applauded, the king presented the boy with the prize purse. Kneeling before the manger, the boy was heard to say, "Baby Jesus, You love my people, and I love You. When You become a man, I will serve You."

Lord, I do believe the greatest is love. Amen.

The Bliss of the Season

It may be a bit old-fashioned—the word *bliss*—but it does describe a Christmas happiness and joy that is downright heavenly.

Imaginative retellings of Jesus' birth have described all of heaven abuzz with excitement over the coming birth of God's Son. He'd be a flesh-and-blood little boy, with a beautiful mother and a caring earthly guardian dad. Is it any wonder that angels and seraphs, and a cherub or two, were blissful in their anticipation?

There's no doubt that bliss describes the excitement a modern child feels at Christmas. And isn't it the emotion we all experience because of a "holy Infant so tender and mild"?

The Christmas family gathering may not be all bliss, but at its heart is the kind of love that's only found with family.

MY FAMILY

The book of the generation of Jesus Christ,
the son of David, the son of Abraham.

MATTHEW 1:1

*H*eavenly Father, most folks admit that if they read the Bible at all, they most certainly don't peruse the first chapter of Matthew—at least not the first seventeen verses—a most impressive who's-who list of Bible greats, all of whom reside in Jesus' family tree.

While few families have their lineage on display around the table at Christmas dinner, every sibling, cousin, parent, and great-great-great grandfather is there, thanks to heritage and DNA. The gene-and-chromosome factor was less important to Jesus, but God-directed heritage and purpose were paramount.

Lord, I realize family is more than a bloodline. When we encircle our table this year, I pray that we will see Jesus' traits in one another. May we recognize our relationship to You, our heavenly Father. Amen.

MY FAMILY

Jesus. . .said, [Allow] the little children to come
unto me. . .for of such is the kingdom of God.
MARK 10:14

Lord, what is more delightful than a baby's first Christmas? It's such a precious time for family photos and admiring the new one. Old rifts and family problems can dissolve into tearful "remember whens."

First Lady Barbara Bush revealed, "To us, family means putting your arms around each other and being there." The hugs are delightful, but the "being there" is what really makes a family a family.

Christmases will come and go. The newborn will have a first day of school. There'll be moments of pride and laughter, but so can there be times when children disappoint, and cause sorrow. But as the old song declares, "through it all," the family is there.

Father, regardless of where we are child-wise, help us make this Christmas a season to pull the family closer. Let embraces replace animosity, and may childlike faith in You reign. Amen.

MY FAMILY

There is a friend that sticketh closer than a brother.

PROVERBS 18:24

*H*eavenly Father, sibling relationships of the brotherly variety are like few others. An only child has never experienced the give-and-take of sharing a bedroom and parents, along with competing in sport and female attention.

Brothers can recall Christmas mornings when size, weight, and supposed cost of their gifts were thoroughly compared, while a sister sibling couldn't care less.

If brothers are such rival creatures in the family circle, why does the ancient proverb compare them to a good friendship? If the proverb had been composed in Jesus' day, the initial *f* would have been capitalized. Today Christian friendship includes our Brother Redeemer, Jesus.

Father, keep Your hand on each person in my family circle so that we will stick close to one another. Amen.

MY FAMILY

He will bless them that fear the Lord,
both small and great. The Lord shall increase
you more and more, you and your children.
Psalm 115:13–14

Father God, the quiet moments parents share at their child's cradle are a study in hopes and dreams.

In long ago Bethlehem Mary and her faithful Joseph must have looked down at their baby in His mother's arms and reminded each other of the angel's promises for their boy: He shall be great. . .Son of the Highest. . .Savior. . .He would save His people from their sins.

While no other parents can dream the dreams of Jesus' family, ours have rich promise and possibilities: the Lord shall bless you and your children more and more. . .they shall be taught by the Lord. . .they may walk in truth. . . the possibility of everlasting life. . . . Above all, they will see God.

Speak to my family, Lord, both young and old; let us see that Your blessings can be ours. Amen.

MY FAMILY

By faith Noah. . .prepared an ark
to the saving of his [family].
HEBREWS 11:7

*F*ather, according to Your plan, the birth of Jesus, like any child's entrance into the world, was a mother-centered event. But no one should minimize Joseph's role as Mary's brave protector, and Jesus' non-Father dad. As the boy grew, Joseph was the parent who taught the skills of manhood, including the proper use of hammer and saw.

It seems He was a proficient carpenter, causing a neighbor to remark that Jesus was a carpenter, and the son of Joseph.

One of the legends about Jesus' boyhood describes Joseph helping Him build a miniature Noah's ark and Jesus' observation, "I would do everything I could to save our family."

Lord, even at Christmas it's difficult to leave Jesus in the manger. Because He came into the world with purpose, it is necessary to look toward Easter, when Jesus did do "everything" to save His greater family. Amen.

MY FAMILY

Let us do good unto all men, especially unto
them who are of the [family] of faith.
GALATIANS 6:10

*H*eavenly Father, the apostle Paul and Jesus never met, except in a vision. He was not a visitor to the Bethlehem stable, nor did he interview the shepherds after their momentous introduction to the Son of God.

Still, the apostle who evidently had no kin, chose to describe believers as comprising a family—a family of faith. Father, that's a most appropriate metaphor. Father, You welcome the homeless celebrating Christmas in a shelter and the sophisticate and the orphan into Your family. At Christmas and always, Your arms are wide open to "whosoever believeth" in You.

> *O holy Child of Bethlehem descend on us, we pray.*
> *Cast out our sin and enter in;*
> *Be born in us today.*
> PHILLIPS BROOKS

Amen.

MY FAMILY

God setteth the solitary in families.

PSALM 68:6

eavenly Father, this Christmas help me to remember "the solitary." According to a newer translation, the psalmist is declaring that the lonely people have their families to pull them out of their aloneness.

The lonely folks represent the powerless, those who are out of step, the quiet and introspective. Their families are responsible for circling the wagons of love and protection.

Christmas is generally the holiday of togetherness and celebration. It's pleasing that You, Father, have taken into consideration those who may need special attention. Thanks be to families for providing it—if at times in boisterous ways. Amen.

MY FAMILY

And thou, child, shalt. . .
give light to them that sit in darkness.
LUKE 1:76, 79

*L*ord, Your servant Luke's phrase, "that sit in darkness," paints a picture of the hundreds of thousands of people who have lost their electricity during a stormy night. When a Gulf Coast hurricane snaps off electricity on Christmas Eve, thousands of kids sit in the dark waiting for Santa Claus. Their stockings are all hung on their chimneys with care, but without the accompaniment of light or TV.

That's when an inventive mother goes to work lighting the decorative candles strewn around the room, causing her impatient daughter to remark, "How come it's taken so long for the light to get here?"

So, Father, when I ask, Why did it take so long for the Light of the world to make His appearance? I am led to Galatians 4:4: "When the fulness of the time was come, God sent forth his Son." That's sufficient for me. I praise You for Your perfect plans. Amen.

MY FAMILY

There was in the days of Herod the king of Judaea,
a certain priest name Zacharias. . .and his wife was. . .
Elisabeth. . . . They both were now well stricken in years.
LUKE 1:5, 7

God in heaven, as You well know, the full miracle of the Christmas story has a parallel family connection involving Zacharias, a priest, and his wife Elizabeth, Mary's elderly kinsman. The third character in this near-unbelievable drama is another angel with more God-ordained news— ancient Elizabeth was pregnant with John, who would prepare the way for his cousin, Jesus.

Not many (if any) families can sit around their Christmas dinner table boasting such royal connections, however most will probably have elderly loved ones in the circle. While no angel announcements will be expected, the family seniors will have rich reminiscences of Christmases past and stories of their wee ones in their cradles.

Lord, thank You for keeping Your hand on the aging in our families. Give them the physical and mental strength to share Your goodness with us. Amen.

MY FRIENDS

Behold. . .they shall call his name Emmanuel,
which being interpreted is, God with us.
MATTHEW 1:23

*F*ather, for many of us to celebrate Your Son's birth in style, we need friends around us. Not in place of family, but we need folks with whom there's comfort, who share a love for this season. I believe the greatest host gift any friend could ever give are the words "Don't sweat it, I'm with you."

All of Your creation has its less-than-bliss-filled moments—and for some, Christmas can magnify their aloneness. That's where supportive friends, with a strong handshake or a hug, remind me that they are there when needed.

Not many name their sons Emmanuel anymore. But You did, and I know why. He is still with us. Proverbs declares that "He is a Friend who sticks closer than a brother"—I say, maybe even closer.

Lord, I want to be Jesus to a friend this season. Give me insight to know what I can do and be. Amen.

MY FRIENDS

A friend loveth at all times.
PROVERBS 17:17

*L*ord, friendship lies in loving, rather than in being loved. That sounds a lot like the unconditional love You have for me, and what Jesus expects from me toward other people.

In our defense, some folks sign almost all their Christmas cards with "Lovingly" or something similar—even to those they hardly know. And some of us take the prize for hugging and warmly shaking hands with complete strangers at church. How much more do You expect?

Oh yes, the scripture states a *friend* loves, not an acquaintance or fellow pew-sitter. Some people might say, "But, Lord, I love everybody, it's just my nature." But friendliness doesn't necessarily involve the heart and love. Facebook and Twitter are friendly, but heartfelt friendship stems from You. Lord, thanks for good friends who love me in spite of my flaws. Help me to be such a friend in return. Amen.

MY FRIENDS

Let love [friendship]. . .
be kindly affectioned one to another.
ROMANS 12:9–10

*H*eavenly Father, relationships with family and friends can become complicated, especially during Christmas entertaining. Between the in-law situations, personal problems between friends, politics, and religious differences, sometimes the best bet is to go to Grandma's and let her cope.

I like the apostle Paul's phrase "kindly affectioned" or "Be devoted and faithful to one another." That's Your reminder that kindness and affection go hand in hand. You don't have one without the other!

Father, before I ask You to make someone "kindly affectionate" toward me, I promise to use this friend-saturated season for strengthening the friendships that I have allowed to become strained. Amen.

MY FRIENDS

Let love [friendship] be. . .rejoicing. . .patient. . .
distributing to the necessity of saints; given to hospitality.
ROMANS 12:9, 12–13

*L*ord, Your requirements of loving friendship are personal. Those believers in Rome had a lot to live up to as friends, and so do each of us.

The following anonymous lines were found scribbled on a paper that was blowing down a London street on Christmas Eve during the First World War: "My friend: Did you know you were brave, did you know you were strong? . . . Did you know there was one leaning hard? . . . Did you know that I waited and listened and prayed. . . ? And was cheered by your simple words. . . Did you know I grew stronger and better because I touched your shoulder? My friend."

Father, may the words of my mouth and the meditations of my heart be influences for good among my friends today. Amen.

MY FRIENDS

Do thy diligence to come before winter.
2 TIMOTHY 4:21

*F*ather God, everyone wants to go back home for Christmas. There's something about being with family and friends for the holidays that makes everything okay.

A prison cell is no place to celebrate Christmas or any other day, especially for one who is doing Your work. Paul, the missionary apostle, found a prison cell his home on at least three occasions. While December 25 was not yet declared a holiday, he, too, wanted to be comforted with friendship before winter. He was lonely. So he begged his son-like friend Timothy to come to him with "diligence."

Other such scenarios will be played out for thousands of believers in countries where Christ has few friends. The Herods of our day are still attempting to stamp out the influence of the King of kings. Just as Paul lost his life for Christ's sake in Rome, so it may be for twenty-first-century martyrs. Lord, protect and comfort those who are being persecuted for Your name's sake this Christmas. Amen.

MY FRIENDS

Every man is a friend to him that giveth gifts.
PROVERBS 19:6

*L*ord, television advertising can wear thin during the Christmas season. The shopping network can persuade us that we need every bauble and time-saving innovation known to humankind—and each salesman has solved the problem of those impossible-to-buy-for friends and relatives.

It seems that Christmas-gift pitchmen have taken Proverbs 19:6 to heart. Father, I enjoy buying thoughtful gifts for my friends to express how much I appreciate them, but I know my closest friends will stick by me even if I have nothing for them to unwrap.

Father, thank You for the friends You've placed in my life. But most of all, I'm glad that I can say I have a friend in Your Son, Jesus, who gave me the greatest gift—a future with You in heaven. Amen.

The Son of man is come eating and drinking. . .
a friend of publicans and sinners.

LUKE 7:34

*H*eavenly Father, I'm not sure how many publicans will be at the Christmas festivities this year, but there certainly will be sinners. That's the comfortable thing about Jesus, He's "at home" with people like me.

If Jesus were making a guest list, there wouldn't be a discussion about reputation, vocation, ethnicity, or state of grace—He'd be guided by Your "whosoever will." There might be some uncomfortable sinners at the table, but their Host would be right at home.

Lord, while our homes are beautifully bedecked with glistening tinsel and boughs of evergreen, prepare our minds, as well as our hearts, to be a friend to all who enter our lives in the season of "goodwill and peace." May the sweet fragrance of friendship be as appetizing as the scents coming from our kitchens. Amen.

MY FRIENDS

This is my beloved, and this is my friend.
SONG OF SOLOMON 5:16

*L*ord, there's something winsome about Solomon's friendship with the person he loved. It's nearly a foreshadowing of Jesus' high view of friendship.

When our partner under the mistletoe is both our beloved and our friend, we have the best of both worlds.

A Christmas shopper was asked by a jewelry salesclerk, "Is this for your 'friend' or your wife?" The shopper replied, "Both." "Oh, then you want two of them?" said the clerk. "No," answered the customer, "one will do. You see my wife is my very best friend."

Lord, I thank You that You have sacrificially and lovingly chosen the church as Your bride. Help me remain faithful to You throughout my life so that when You return You'll say, "This is my beloved, and this is my friend." Amen

MY FRIENDS

I have called you friends.

JOHN 15:15

God, many people have happy memories of their childhood best friends. The basis of a good friendship is loyalty. Best friends stick up for each other. They choose each other first when dividing up for a game. Sometimes they can even be talked into sharing their snacks. Youthful best friendships are not complicated. They just are.

Childhood friendship is as simple as childhood faith. When children sing, "Yes, Jesus loves me," they mean it with all their hearts. Lord, as I child I felt as close to You as I did to my best friend. Please renew in my heart that childlike faith and trust in You. Amen.

MY GIVING

They [wise men from the east] fell down, and worshipped
him: and when they had opened their treasures, they pre-
sented unto him gifts; gold, and frankincense and myrrh.

MATTHEW 2:11

*H*eavenly Father, pastors say that You are
omniscient—that You know everything. I'm not. I make
to-do lists, and I can't foresee what my future will be.

I've wondered what went through Mary's mind when
wise and king-like men offered her little Son those overwhelming gifts of gold, frankincense, and myrrh. Were
You preparing her for what to expect in the years ahead?
Gold for a King? Frankincense for His divinity? Myrrh as a
foreshadowing of the cross?

Father, I'm discovering that Christmas is not so much
about the apps and iPads, but the reassurance that my day-
by-day gifts to friends and family have eternal value. I invite Your Holy Spirit to empower me for eternal gifting to
those I care for. No batteries required. Amen.

MY GIVING

Silver and Gold have I none; but such as I have give I
thee: In the name of Jesus of Nazareth rise up and walk.
ACTS 3:6

*H*eavenly Father, many of us during this shopping season have the short-in-cash reaction that prompted
Peter's response to the lame man sitting at the temple gate.
The beggar thought that money was the solution to his
problems, but the fisherman disciple didn't have silver or
gold to give.

The old beggar's "gift wants" may have been pretty
minimal, but wise Peter went to the heart of the matter—
he gifted him by healing the man's lameness in the name of
Jesus.

Spending is a Christmas custom that can get out of
hand. Giving is a selfless experience that when performed
in the name of Jesus, can become life changing for the one
who receives, and for the person who gives.

Father, give me Your mind in my gift giving this
Christmas. Remind me to send a prayer along with each
package, and when possible, let my selections reflect Jesus.
Amen.

MY GIVING

It is more blessed to give than to receive.

ACTS 20:35

*L*ord, some parents may try quoting this scripture to their offspring before a visit to Macy's Toyland: "Remember, dear, it's more blessed to give than to receive!"

Dr. Spock, the controversial pediatrician of the sixties, has been paraphrased as telling parents that the spirit of generosity and giving must be demonstrated to children as early as possible if they are to grow up into givers and not takers.

Jesus' statement has also become an established pre-offering reading in church ritual around the world. Father, at Christmas and throughout the year, I want this phrase to become part of my stewardship. Amen.

Charge them that are rich in this world, that they be not highminded, nor trust in uncertain riches, but in the living God, who giveth us richly all things to enjoy.

1 TIMOTHY 6:17

*H*eavenly Father, how do we celebrate Christmas with our country and the whole world in such an upsetting state? Where do believers turn for reassurance?

One of the secrets for a joyful Christmas isn't hidden away awaiting gift wrap in a back closet somewhere. This secret, 1 Timothy 6:17, is no secret at all, and You gave it for our encouragement as well, not just for the first-century believers—don't trust in riches but in You, Lord.

They were penned by the apostle for his son in the faith, Timothy, as a charge for the persecuted church at a time when prison and death awaited many who claimed Christ.

Their message of encouragement at Christmas is Enjoy! You give us all things. You are rich in Your giving. You are our source of every good and perfect gift. Amen.

MY GIVING

Thanks be unto God for his unspeakable gift.

2 Corinthians 9:15

*L*ord, some of us still feel keenly about giving thanks before we eat, whether in a café or at our own kitchen table. The menu doesn't dictate the need, but the heart does. Somehow You have planted that want-to within us, and we thank You for it.

But some gift receivers don't express their "thank you." Parents often have to prod their children into writing those post-Christmas obligatory thank-you notes to away-from-here aunts and uncles for presents that often didn't meet their expectations.

So, how do You feel about heaping upon us every good and perfect gift beyond our expectations, and receiving nary an expression of thanks and appreciation?

Lord, forgive us for thoughtlessly taking for granted all that You give us. Our best gift giving can never compare to Your gift of Jesus. Amen.

MY GIVING

*If ye then, being evil, know how to give good gifts unto
your children, how much more shall your Father which is
in heaven give good things to them that ask him.*

MATTHEW 7:11

Father, children begin dropping hints for Christmas
gifts in earnest after Thanksgiving. There are various tech-
niques, and the hinting is a game with hoped-for conse-
quences.

The appropriate time for opening gifts can also be a
hot debate. There are the Christmas Eve openers and the
Christmas morning openers—some newlyweds have nearly
called it quits over this very issue.

And the origin of all this? The birth of a boy. No one
knows for sure the exact date of His birthday, or the exact
time. The most important fact of His birth is that He is
"more than any good gift we could ever dream of." And it
was Your gift to us.

Lord, I want my giving to be meaningful and appreci-
ated, but how much more important is it to recognize that
Your gift was perfect. Amen.

MY GIVING

Give us this day our daily bread.
MATTHEW 6:11

*H*eavenly Father, there are few aromas more mouthwateringly wonderful than baking bread. And the things that a good baker can do with a yeasty dough mixed with some Christmassy ingredients can be stupendous.

It's good that Jesus selected bread as one of life's necessities. Those who heard realized that it represented the stuff of life that You would give to those who asked. At the Last Supper, Jesus broke bread with His disciples in recognition of His coming death.

As bread is passed at Christmas dinner this year, I will hold it in my hand and silently thank You for providing everything that I need. Amen.

MY GIVING

Blessed is he that considereth the poor:
the LORD will deliver him in time of trouble.

PSALM 41:1

ather God, it's difficult to discuss poverty in this season of the year. No one likes a guilt trip at Christmas. It can be rather easy to shift our gazes another direction at the sound of a bell ringer, or to hang up on phone solicitors. But to be confronted by homelessness and hunger that's all around us?—that's tough.

There's an appealing promise attached to this psalmist's quote—deliverance when trouble comes knocking at my door. Are You offering me an insurance policy? To be "blessed" and "delivered" is a big deal.

Lord, help me to recall that You work through us. We are Your hands.

The poet Kagawa writes, "Penniless. . .a while without food I can live; but it breaks my heart to know I cannot give." And my heart prays, "I can give; show me how." Amen.

MY GIVING

No good thing will he withhold.
PSALM 84:11

*L*ord, the great bank of heaven must overflow with available assets, but where do the deposits come from? It's sincerely doubtful that the old song "Pennies from Heaven" is a true picture of those divine assets. I prefer the lyrics of the church song by Annie J. Flint:

> *His love has no limit, His grace has no measure,*
> *His power no boundary known unto men;*
> *But out of His infinite riches in Jesus*
> *He giveth, and He giveth, and He giveth again.*

Dear Lord, I want to reflect Your example in my small way; lay upon my heart the spirit of grace-filled giving. Amen.

MY LORD

*Where is he that is born King of the Jews? for we have
seen his star in the east, and are come to worship him.*

MATTHEW 2:2

Heavenly Father, even with a tin ear, many people confess that some of Handel's grand and glorious *Messiah* energizes them to the degree that they're tempted to pull on a robe and join right in.

By the time the choir gets to the "King of kings, and Lord of lords!" part, everyone's on their feet wiping away tears realizing the truth of Jesus' lordship. It's all overwhelming!

We who don't live in a monarchy probably have no great sense of awe and reverence for the expression "My Lord." When shepherds saw the baby King, they probably knelt at the manger. When the magi found the child, they fell down and worshipped Him. It may have been the first time "My Lord and my God" was ever uttered.

Father and Lord, may my Christmas experience include wonderment for Jesus' lordship. May He reign in my life "Forever and ever. Hallelujah." Amen.

MY LORD

Trust in the LORD with all thine heart;
and lean not unto thine own understanding.

PROVERBS 3:5

God, Christmas shopping decisions are probably not a matter of high priority to You, but it certainly exerts pressure on a lot of us this time of year. Some of us have trouble with "leaning on our own understanding"; in other words, we need help making up our minds.

I want to trust You in every single nook and cranny of my life, in all the decisions that are much bigger than picking out gifts. It's interesting that we turn so readily to friends and all kinds of promise-making hucksters, but so often we're too slow to trust You. I suppose it's partially due to the absentee lord of the manor syndrome—out of sight, out of mind. But that's why You sent Your Son and the blessed Holy Spirit.

Lord, my God, You are not far off, You are here. Direct my path in the ways of righteousness. Amen.

MY LORD

There is but one God, the Father. . .
and one Lord Jesus Christ.

1 CORINTHIANS 8:6

*F*ather God, the importance of calling You "Lord" cannot be overstated. The apostle Paul took that to heart and often referred to Your Son as the Lord Jesus Christ: "Lord," because He is our source of power; "Jesus," because He saves people from their sins; "Christ," because He is Messiah.

The Bethlehem shepherds observed baby Jesus and accepted His lordship because of the angel's announcement. That was all they had to go on. It's doubtful that the baby in the manger looked any different than their children at home. In a way, He was one of them, but still, they knew Jesus was Lord. They rejoiced in the fact.

Father God, I pray that the lordship of Jesus will be acknowledged throughout this Yuletide season—and beyond. Amen.

MY LORD

Delight thyself also in the LORD,
and he shall give thee the desires of thine heart.

PSALM 37:4

Heavenly Father, "the desires of thine heart"—
what a gracious promise, especially this time of year. And
it is delivered with such assurance. It might be easy to take
advantage of Your generosity, Lord. In this materialistic
season of Christmas, it's good to remember that we must
delight in You before we consider the desires of our hearts.

It's not surprising that the word *delight* is coupled
with the word *desires*—so how do people delight them-
selves in You? The most basic definition of *delight* is "joy."
And we can only experience Your joy through closeness.

Dear Lord, let me know the areas of my life where I
need to be closer to You, then I'll leave the desires of my
heart up to You. Amen.

MY LORD

Every tongue should confess that Jesus Christ is Lord,
to the glory of God.
PHILIPPIANS 2:11

*L*ord, often we don't take advantage of the opportunities we have to put in a good word for You. We may be nervous about it, but nothing is keeping us from taking a one-person initiative to confess that Jesus Christ is Lord, in friendly ways.

There's no better time of year to confess Jesus as Lord than at Christmas. Kids' teachers, regardless of faith, welcome cards and small gifts with short notes of appreciation. You bless Christmas cookies delivered to fire and police stations with a holiday scripture attached. Confessing Jesus to "the choir" is fine, but I know that You want me to open my heart to a wider community.

Lord, give me a creative mind to find ways to say, "Thank you" and "Jesus loves you" during this Christmas season. Amen.

MY LORD

Ye serve the Lord Christ.
COLOSSIANS 3:24

*F*ather, why can't Christmas be all joy and good times? Why must there be disaster and unhappiness? Card companies have even developed a line of Christmas cards for those in the throes of tragedy. Maybe the exclamation, "Come Thou quickly Lord Jesus!" has relevance today.

When a child snuggles up close and asks, "Why did Jesus let my auntie die?" is there a Christmas answer? When a brother in the faith loses a job during this season, how much comfort is there in the sweet by and by?

The guarantees found in serving You are not always "delights," but they are assurances. The boy in the manger became the risen Christ. He promises, "Lo, I am with you always." Father, when I am unable to voice reasons and solutions, I want to fall back on the knowledge that You will never leave me. Amen.

MY LORD

This man shall be the peace.
MICAH 5:5

*G*od, the Old Testament fairly explodes in its anticipation of the Lord Jesus—the Messiah so long awaited. It's an eye-opener to read the prophets knowing what we know on this side of Bethlehem.

At that time the world desperately looked for a Lord of Peace. Isaiah called Him the Prince of Peace. Can there be any prayer more repeated than for world peace?

Henry Wadsworth Longfellow's nineteenth-century "Bells on Christmas Day" expresses such a longing for peace:

And in despair I bowed my head.
"There is no peace on earth" I said,
"For hate is strong, and mocks the song
Of peace on earth goodwill to men."

Mr. Longfellow hoped for the cessation of war, but the battles continue to rage. So, Lord, where is the promised peace? It's in the hearts of those who accept the Prince of Peace. Amen.

MY LORD

My soul doth magnify the Lord, and my spirit
hath rejoiced in God my Saviour.
LUKE 1:46–47

*H*eavenly Father, in the first chapter of Luke, the
verses titled "The Song of Mary" (verses 46–55), is found
some of the most beautifully expressed words and phrases
ever spoken in worship.

Her praise is directed to You and expresses her depen-
dence on the "Mighty One" who has done great things for
her. What she says of You would one day be said of the
child she bore.

Luke's beautifully quiet description of Mary's visit
with her kinswoman Elizabeth underscores the young vir-
gin's awe and acceptance of the angel's announcement.
Lord, I, too, praise You for the great things You have done
for me. Amen.

MY LORD

Thou shalt love the Lord thy God with all thy heart,
and with all thy soul, and with all thy mind.

MATTHEW 22:37

ather God, how many times have children answered the parental question, "How much do you love
me?" with a hug around the neck and a "With all my
heart." That's bliss.

According to Matthew, there are no halfhearted re-
sponses in what You, Lord, expect from us, Your children.
No peck on the cheek will do. Loving You consumes *all*
the heart, *all* the soul, and *all* the mind. It's quite straight-
forward; You aren't content with part of me, and it isn't
Christmas-only closeness—the kind that is more interested
in rewards than a spontaneous hug around the neck.

Lord of life, there are so many *things* I love, and I
get so wrapped up in them. Maybe my love for You isn't
always wholehearted. Help me use this sacred time to draw
closer and to express my love for the lordship of Christ.
Amen.

The Blessing of the Season

The blessings of Christmas cannot be contained by any gift box: the excitement of little kids; the smiles of the elderly as their loved ones open hand-crocheted crafts; the sudden rush of emotion while holding a lighted candle and singing, "Silent night, holy night"; the love on the faces of family and friends around a dinner table after a year of personal difficulties; the hopeful gleam in every eye while anticipating an absentee's soon return.

It was Charles Dickens's iconic Tiny Tim who reminded his family, "God bless us, everyone!" And it's John, Jesus' beloved disciple, who reminds us of God's blessings in this season and all the others: "Blessing, and glory. . . honour, and power. . .be unto our God for ever and ever" (Revelation 7:12).

LOVE

Behold what manner of love the Father hath bestowed
upon us, that we should be called the sons of God.

1 JOHN 3:1

*H*eavenly Father, few things are as wonderful as
the three words, "I love you." And who better than John,
the beloved disciple, to remind the world that You are love,
and because of that love we can be called Your children.

Father, sometimes I wonder why You take notice of
me. I feel small and insignificant. But I know that You see
when a little bird falls, so I know You care even more for
me. I praise You for sending Jesus. Your love is so great
that You didn't hold back even Your Son. Lord, please use
me to point my loved ones who don't yet know You to the
cross.

> *Love came down at Christmas*
> *Love all lovely, Love Divine.*
> *Love was born at Christmas*
> *Star and angels gave the sign.*
>
> CHRISTINA ROSSETTI

Amen.

LOVE

A new commandment I give unto you,
That ye love one another.
JOHN 13:34

ather, the family refrigerator door takes on another magnet during the Yuletide season—a new item joins grocery lists and kids' artwork; it now bears a chore list: "Get Done before Christmas Eve!" The exclamation mark puts fear in the hearts of readers—a bit like writing "Or else!"

Chores and commands can be a bit difficult to accept, especially by the young. That's why many such directives carry the softening ID, "Love, Mom." Besides, when Christmas is involved, love carries a lot of influence.

At a gathering of His disciples in an upper room, Jesus realized that the work ahead allowed no room for animosity within the ranks of His followers. In John's Gospel Jesus gives them a new command: "Love one another." He follows with the explanation, "so you will be recognized as My disciples."

Lord, during the stressful Christmas season, when we're tempted to lash out at one another, help us remember Your charge to love. Amen.

LOVE

Herein is love, not that we loved God,
but that he loved us, and sent his Son.
1 JOHN 4:10

God, at this year's Christmas dinners, how many wishbone-breaking rituals will involve unspoken yearnings for a love that will reunite families and mend broken relationships?

It may be a naive question; but where are the contemporary examples of true selfless love? The kind seldom seen on movie screens and that's not dependent on extravagant gifts.

Need anyone look further than the example of Your selfless love, wonderfully portrayed in the ageless narrative of Jesus' supernatural birth.

But will the guests at a holiday dinner relate to Your love? Will the estranged find acceptance? Can the down-on-their-luck identify? Will the unloved feel loved? Yes to all on one condition: that believers around the table allow Your unconditional love to energize their hearts—that they will demonstrate the love that brought Jesus into our world. Please, let it be so at my table this year. Amen.

LOVE

If we love one another, God dwelleth in us.

1 John 4:12

*H*eavenly Father, an Advent calendar used to be a colorful necessity for counting down the days to Christmas. It had twenty-four numbered doors that were daily opened in sequence to reveal Bible verses.

One verse that appeared often was "God dwelleth in us," which often prodded children to ask their doctors, "Can you hear God in there?" This encouraged the response, "Only if you love others."

Christmas is an ideal time to take inventory of Your presence within us. No doubt such a checklist would ask about personal quiet time, involvement in corporate worship, stewardship, and the like. But "Do you love others?" would lead off the questionnaire.

Father, I know I have committed my life to You, but sometimes I need to be reminded that my love for others is evidence that You live in me. Amen.

LOVE

The fruit of the Spirit is love.

GALATIANS 5:22

*L*ord, the natural decor of Christmas can be the most beautiful: pungent evergreen, prickly dark green holly and its scarlet berries, brilliant poinsettia plants, and sweet-smelling paper whites bursting from their crinkly bulbs. All are right at home amid the sparkles and glow.

There was a time when Christmas meant oranges, the large bright orange variety that often found its way into the toe of fireplace-hung stockings.

While the grocer has sweet fruit of every kind, even in the dead of winter, Your Word teaches that there are spiritual fruit or traits that are the result of the abiding presence of Your Spirit in our lives. The fruits include joy, kindness, self-control, and patience. But the first spiritual fruit is love—the self-giving kind that's not dependent on circumstance or reward. Father, may the spiritual fruits of Your presence ripen in my life. Amen.

LOVE

Pure religion and undefiled before. . .the Father is this,
To visit the fatherless and widows in their affliction.

JAMES 1:27

God, it's so easy to love our own, but sometimes so, so difficult to reach out to the less attractive and the problematic, even at Christmas. Most of us can love without qualification the folks who sit around us in church. We give financially to missions and compassionate ministries and help support kids in other parts of the world. All done without a qualm or complaint.

Unlike Ebenezer Scrooge, it's often not the money, it's the giving of my self—my time and energy—when there is no tangible hope of return. In the spirit of James's scripture, I really want my faith to be pure and authentic, and I don't want You to think I'm shirking, but sometimes I struggle in times of affliction.

Loving Father, forgive me for my selfishness and create in me a clean heart of love. Amen.

LOVE

There is no fear in love;
but perfect love casteth out fear.
1 JOHN 4:18

*F*ather in heaven, fear and love seem poles apart, though most of us have experienced both. We love our parents, but as children we sometimes feared their correction.

Children often want to help with the tree decorating at Christmas. And many ornaments have shattered after falling from their little fingers. Lord, that's Your cue for perfect love to take over. You know that anger will never conquer fear, only love can do that. The shards of our favorite ornaments are a testing point.

Father, I praise You that I have no fear of God's judgment, because genuine love affirms my salvation. Amen.

LOVE

That their hearts might be comforted. . .
knit together in love.
Colossians 2:2

*H*eavenly Father, a house full of family at Christmas sounds like a complete delight, except when perfect love is not the overarching connection between people.

Counselors have advised soon-to-be husbands, "Love says, 'I see you, I hear you, I know you are there.'" And then added, "Works on the in-laws, too."

Christ-like love acknowledges the worth of others. An old hymn says, "In Christ there is no East or West. . .but one great brotherhood"—that included even muddy shepherds and wise old men.

Lord, I want to do some heart knitting this Christmas. Fill my house with an aroma of Your presence; give me the energy and desire to be Christ to all I come in contact with. Amen.

LOVE

My little children, let us not love in word,
neither in tongue; but in deed and in truth.

1 JOHN 3:18

*L*ord, as busy as You must be, it's amazing how You have always been proactive in bringing to pass the most intimate and life-changing events in history.

Your loving care for the Nazareth family in Bethlehem is most certainly evidence of Your planning: The generous innkeeper could have said no and slammed the door shut. The shepherds out on the hillside could have thrown another log on the fire and said, "First thing in the morning." The wise men from the East could have gone home the same way they had come, causing all kinds of calamity.

John strikes a responsive note with his definition of love; it's not shown by the number of times I say, "I love you." Nor is it the quantity of Valentines I send. Father, let my love be an active expression of authentic deeds and actions. Amen.

PEACE

Peace I leave with you, my peace I give unto you.
JOHN 14:27

ather, it's easy to sing the words "sleep in heavenly peace" and see them as nothing more than just Christmas-card sentiment. Lord, is it realistic to believe that our world can ever bring about a complete cessation of war and selfish aggression? It's one thing for sheep herders to accept the angel's declaration of a peaceful earth, but it's another thing for little children in war-torn places to experience "heavenly peace." While we may never live in peace here on earth, I thank You that my heart is filled with the peace of Your Spirit.

A once popular song says, "Let there be peace on earth, and let it begin in me." But, Lord, I know that peace begins in You. You promised to fill us with peace that passes understanding. Father, give me faith and opportunity to share the gift of peace. Amen.

PEACE

Thou wilt keep him in perfect peace,
whose mind is stayed on thee.
ISAIAH 26:3

*H*eavenly Father, it's tough for children to get settled down to sleep on Christmas Eve. "Sugarplums" dance in their wee little heads, probably the result of too many goodies in their tummies.

The wonderful anticipation of Christmas, all wrapped up in the promise of peace, can keep adults awake, too. Difficult memories of other Yules in other times can keep sleep from coming, as can the longing for personal peace on earth.

Father, is "perfect peace" a prophetic promise that has not yet been born? Help me to keep my mind focused on You, and I pray that the Prince of Peace will make Himself known to me and mine in a greater way this Christmas. Amen.

PEACE

The fruit of the spirit is love, joy, peace.

GALATIANS 5:22

*F*ather God, for some, peace brings to mind a halt in battle; for others, it's the atmosphere of a favorite vacation spot; while still others recall an idyllic childhood. While these are examples of outward calm, inner peace is a gift that is achieved only through Your Holy Spirit.

Father, Your Christmas promise of peace on earth seems impossible at times. Some have come to the conclusion that the angel's message needed a disclaimer: "This offer is valid only for hungry hearts who truly seek Him." Lord, please bring to fruition in my life the inner peace that comes with the presence of Your Spirit. Amen.

PEACE

Blessed are the peacemakers:
for they shall be called the children of God.

MATTHEW 5:9

*H*eavenly Father, Jesus taught His disciples and a multitude of the curious on a hillside in Galilee the rewards of living in peace.

His words of peace have the ring of a Bethlehem angel's, but He urged His followers to take the reins and become peacemakers. Judging by the audience, He was not suggesting a professional team of attorneys or labor negotiators, but everyday people like us.

This, the seventh Beatitude, comes with a promise— peacemakers will be called Your children. If the pure in heart will see You, then those who proclaim and work for peace are Your children—with pure hearts. Father, as Your child, give me the peace that surpasses all understanding, so that I in turn can influence others for the same peace. Amen.

PEACE

Let us therefore follow after the things which make for
peace, and things wherewith one may edify another.
ROMANS 14:19

*G*od, war and unrest edify no one. That's a truth that
moms try to drum into the heads of their youngsters. In
Sunday school children learn that at Jesus' birth jealousy
and fear stole the lives of countless children—because a
king feared the King of kings.

For the kids' sake, Lord, and for the sake of homes
and families across this great land, encourage the practice
of peace. Let our words and deeds be such that they lead
to peace and mutual encouragement. Give us the desire
to move through our world ever conscious of the slogan:
"What would Jesus do, and say, and be?" Amen.

PEACE

[He] came and preached peace to you which were afar off,
and to them that were nigh.

EPHESIANS 2:17

*L*ord of heaven, bid our peace increase; encourage oppression cease; turn the night into peace, and let a new day be born. Give those who battle, far off or nigh, hearts to believe the promise of peace for those who cry.

Good God of blessed peacefulness, make all our warfare end; banish inner battle, purge me of the hated enemy, so to offer a forgiving hand, and grasp as friend to friend.

Lord of blissful day, Redeemer of angry night, undo the shackle of turmoil; plant deep the hope for change; reveal Your stillness strategy on battlefield and hearth; hold close and give remembrance to still Eden's quiet fields, and give the world Your peace, as an everlasting Light.

Lord of all that's light, give us reason this Christmas, to be peace to all who enter our doors or cross our paths. Where there is warfare, let us be peace. Amen.

PEACE

[Jesus] said unto the sea, Peace, be still. And the wind
ceased, and there was a great calm.

MARK 4:39

*H*eavenly Father, when the weather forecast doesn't look good for Christmas travel, and little noses are pressed against the window waiting for Grandma and Grandpa's car to appear, nothing delivers a rush of peace like the words, "They're here!"

In a wind- and wave-tossed sailboat out in the middle of Galilee, nothing lifted the storm of fear like Jesus' calming "Peace, be still." Perhaps an observer from the shore was surprised at the man's command over nature, but there was no surprise among the passengers of the little skiff, they knew their Lord specialized in lifting fear and creating peace.

Father God, it sometimes feels as if my little boat of responsibility is capsizing—especially at this time of year. Please let me hear, "Peace, be still." Amen.

PEACE

Follow peace with all men.
HEBREWS 12:14

*G*od, peace is not a once-and-for-all experience; it's a lot like marriage, it takes work. Married couples understand that at Christmas spousal peace can be in short supply.

Who hasn't had family peace shatter like Aunt Sophie's Waterford stemware when discussing money? Or what well-prepared host doesn't simmer like the boiling potatoes out in the kitchen when hearing, "Oh, I forgot to tell you, I've invited the new guy and his family for dinner tonight"?

The phrase "follow peace" means "make every effort" or "strive" for peace. *Effort* and *strive* are causal words, they are part of a make-it-happen person's discipline. Lord, what was once called a "deep settled peace" is a gift from You. Please let it begin in me. Amen.

PEACE

And thou, child, shalt be called the prophet of the
Highest. . .[Who will] give light to them that sit in
darkness and. . .to guide our feet into the way of peace.
LUKE 1:76, 79

ather God, the Christmas story begins in the chapter before the shepherds and star bit, it starts with an old man named Zacharias, whose elderly wife Elizabeth gave birth to a boy they named John—Jesus' cousin and His forerunner.

Old Zacharias knew Your plan for Your Son. In his song of praise, Zacharias acknowledges that the child Mary bore would "guide our feet in the way of peace."

No one sings Christmas carols about Zacharias's son John, but John the Gospel writer reports that Elizabeth's son was the first to verify Jesus' divinity: "Behold the Lamb of God" (John 1:36).

Father, continue to direct me in the ways of peace. Amen.

HOPE

Every man. . .hath this hope in him.
1 John 3:3

*H*eavenly Father, this Christmas my corner of Your creation is one huge explosion of sparkle and excitement. In nearly every direction are reminders of Christmas peace and love, but too often missing is the promise of hope.

Hope is an uplifting word. Father, use this hymn to encourage me when I feel the stress of the holidays building: "When all around my soul gives way, He then is all my hope and stay." This Christmas I'm counting on You to be my hope!

Lord, to all of us who depend on a hope in Christ to make it through, John's words above remind us that a believer's hope goes beyond Bethlehem and Jesus' first appearance, it is a settling realization that He is coming again. Dear Father, who can ask for a gift better than eternity with You? Amen.

HOPE

I say, through the grace given unto me. . . .
Rejoicing in hope.
ROMANS 12:3, 12

*L*ord, gift-opening time holds all sorts of surprises and hoped-for outcomes. When the fancy wrap is unceremoniously ripped open and anxious givers study first facial reactions, then it's time to ask, "Is it what you hoped for?"

Kids are easy to read, when they get what they hoped for, there's usually a grand explosion of rejoicing. But socially-aware adults have perfected the fine art of present unwrapping with more deliberation. In some cases, stick-on bows are set aside for reuse; ribbon is wound into a neat package for the same reason; Scotch tape is carefully peeled away, allowing tissue paper to be gently smoothed and folded. By the time the box lid is removed, the poised reaction, "Just what I wanted" is applauded by everyone in the circle.

Father, do You have hopes for us? Are we what You've always wanted us to be? Lord, please peel away the shiny outer layers that I present to the world and help me become more like You on the inside. Amen.

HOPE

*Lay hold upon the hope set before us: Which hope we
have as an anchor of the soul, both sure and steadfast.*

HEBREWS 6:18–19

*F*ather, girls love charm bracelets, jingling with silver or gold charms: the cross for faith, a heart for love, and an anchor representing hope. The anchor is what holds a ship safely in position, just like our hope is steadfast, anchored in Your promise of everlasting life.

No doubt, the bracelet's theology doesn't impress twelve-year-olds as much as the attention it draws. To the spiritually young, the anchor of hope reflects the future, while a mature believer realizes, "My hope is based on nothing less, Than Jesus' blood and righteousness."

Father, anchor my life to the hope I have in You. Amen.

∴

HOPE

*Now the God of hope fill you with all joy
and peace in believing, that ye may abound in hope,
through the power of the Holy Ghost.*

ROMANS 15:13

*H*eavenly Father, no one can question the power of Your Holy Spirit working in the lives of young Mary and her espoused husband, Joseph.

During the pre-Bethlehem months, did Joseph ever waver in his faith, or did the angel's assurances provide him with a peaceful heart? As a pregnant teenager, did Mary and her family continue to rejoice in You?

As a contemporary believer, it's a stretch not to wonder if their hope stood up under the testings of neighbors and perhaps even members of their own families. Theirs was a hope or longing for whatever You had in store, a belief in the power of Your Spirit to bring all things to pass.

Father, that's my hope, too. When family or friends become a negative influence in my life, please keep my faith strong and allow me to demonstrate Your love to them. Amen.

HOPE

We through patience and comfort
of the scriptures might have hope.
Romans 15:4

Father God, the family around Mary knew they were to hold fast to their hope in Your Holy Spirit and Your promises. Their confidence and hope was based on the scripture they heard in synagogue on the Sabbath when their rabbi read from Isaiah: "The people that walked in darkness have seen a great light: they that dwell in the land of the shadow of death, upon them hath the light shined" (Isaiah 9:2).

Like their Nazareth neighbors, Mary and her family took comfort and found hope in the scripture. The world waited with patience while Mary and Joseph kept all they had seen and heard and continued their hope in God's promise.

Lord, patience is a virtue, I know, but like a child at Christmas, I am eager for the morning of hope and the answer to long-prayed prayers. Renew my patience while waiting for Your promises to be fulfilled. Amen.

HOPE

We are saved by hope:
but hope that is seen is not hope.
ROMANS 8:24

*L*ord in heaven, there must be a special kind of hope reserved just for Christmas. In a way, this hope has to do with faith. If hope has to be seen and smelled and touched, then maybe it isn't hope (or faith).

Lots of children and parents find their hope quotient increases as Advent moves into Christmastide—when storage closets become off-limits and knowing looks pass between all concerned.

The Bible tells us that we are saved *by* grace, and today's scripture states we are saved *in* hope. Faith and hope are near cousins: the experience demands faith, and the very experience of salvation imparts hope.

Dear Lord, maybe that is part of the Christmas hope quotient. I accept the coming of Jesus in faith, and it fills me with hope. Amen.

HOPE

Thou art my hope, O Lord GOD:
thou art my trust from my youth.

PSALM 71:5

Heavenly Father, "Since my youth, You have been my trust" is a strong confession of hope. But many of us spend our youth thinking that we don't need You. Sometimes we even try to run away from You like Jonah, but that didn't turn out very well for Jonah—and it usually doesn't for us either.

It seems we must reach a point where we are hoping for a life that's better than where we're headed. That's when a want-to-be becomes a believer—when hope becomes trust.

Father, I pray that it doesn't take a wake-up call of whale-like proportions to bring the children and adults in my family to Your saving grace. Show me how to demonstrate the hope of my salvation to them this Christmas season. Amen.

I will give. . .a door of hope.
HOSEA 2:15

*L*ord, celebrating the birth of Christ is a fiesta of hope. In the spirit of Bethlehem, Mexicans observe La Posada with a village reenactment of Mary and Joseph, seeking an open door for the Holy Family. The procession of friends knock on doors seeking a hospitable "innkeeper," who invites them in for a Christmas piñata.

The door metaphor wasn't lost to Old Testament prophets either. They pointed the way to the Messiah and the hope to be found in Jesus, who would later reveal, "I am the door: by me if any man enter in, he shall be saved" (John 10:9).

Father God, to You who invite us into Your house, may my open door and heart bring hope to all who enter in. Amen.

HOPE

*Blessed be the God and Father of our Lord Jesus Christ,
which according to his abundant mercy hath begotten us
again unto a lively hope.*

1 PETER 1:3

ather God, what a welcome verse of scripture, particularly the reference to "lively" hope. It has to be Your grace that encouraged Peter to write a letter that is so filled with hope!

Lively is most certainly an appropriate word for this season of the year. Too often many of us allow less-than-positive thoughts into our brains. At times, all the what-ifs try to overpower living hope. That's the time to hum, "My hope is built on nothing less, than Jesus' blood and righteousness."

I find great hope in Peter's epistles, God, grant that more of it takes root. Amen.

SALVATION

*Whosoever believeth in him [Jesus Christ] should
not perish, but have everlasting life.*
JOHN 3:16

*G*od, in the midst of all this Christmas beauty, busyness, bliss, and blessing, I must express my thanks for all
the gifts You have heaped upon me—the best and greatest
being Jesus. He's the One angels sang about, shepherds
were awed by, wise kings gifted, and an innkeeper nearly
shut out. For more than two thousand years the creative
have used the inspiration of His miraculous birth as subject
matter to entertain and inspire.

Lord, the missing truth of most Christmas seasons is
the *why* of it all. Some think it's to give merchants a better
balance sheet.

No, the reason for Bethlehem is summarized in the
angelic message: "He shall save his people from their sins"
(Matthew 1:21). That's what inspired John to give the
world the most recognized Bible verse of all, John 3:16.
Father, may each of us become one of Your "whosoever."
Amen.

SALVATION

Neither is there salvation in any other:
for there is none other name under heaven given
among men, whereby we must be saved.

ACTS 4:12

*H*eavenly Father, believers realize there's no hocus-pocus magic in the name "Jesus," but according to the pre-Christmas nativity narratives, both Mary and Joseph received distinct instructions for christening Mary's Son—"Name Him Jesus," with the explanation that "He shall save His people."

There's a lot to be saved from today, not the least of which is ourselves. A name alone can't provide salvation, it's what that name stands for. No other means of salvation carries God's seal of approval as does the name Jesus.

An anonymous poet testified, "I know a soul that is steeped in sin, that no man's art can cure; But I know a Name, a wonderful Name, that can make that soul all pure."

And that name is Jesus. Amen.

SALVATION

Behold, now is the day of salvation.

2 CORINTHIANS 6:2

*F*ather, I hope I can get everything done; my gotta-do list has increased since the last time we talked about it. It seems like everything needs doing right now! What's happened to "all is calm, all is bright"?

I suppose this is why some folks find their quiet times so beneficial at Christmas. Even then, my mind still wanders to my gotta-dos. Some Christmased-out people have swapped their chore list for a prayer list, even going so far as assigning names to specific days of the week.

Father, short of buying everybody a Bible this year, help me give my friends and family the secret gift of remembering them in prayer. Amen.

SALVATION

Wherefore, my beloved. . .in my absence,
work out your own salvation with fear and trembling.
PHILIPPIANS 2:12

ather God, there's a lot I'd like to be saved from during this time of year. It would be enjoyable to sit back and look at Christmas through the eyes of innocence, un-clouded by responsibility. Just soaking in the sights and sounds of the season.

But work we must. It's interesting that when the apostle Paul was about to leave for one of his missionary journeys, his well-recognized work ethic surfaced. Like the parent who's holiday bound, Paul leaves instructions of how to carry on in his absence. Buried in the middle of his directives, he reminds those left behind to "work out their own salvation." They'd have to keep on keeping on in their faith.

Father, maturing in Christ is my workout responsibil-ity. I recognize my responsibility for growth in grace and in my likeness to Jesus. Amen.

SALVATION

Put on. . .the helmet of salvation.
EPHESIANS 6:11, 17

*L*ord, believers used to give lapel pins for Christmas. The pins were worn as silent witnesses—indications to the world that the wearers were saved. Others tried wearing a certain kind of hat as an indication of faith, perhaps in compliance with the helmet advice in Philippians. But the helmet in Paul's imagery served two purposes: it was a handsome identification of rank and bravery, plus it protected the head. In the apostle's thinking, salvation, like armor, is our protection from Satan, as well as indicative of whose we are.

Father, I believe that Christmas is a wonderful time to share my personal salvation story. With or without a head covering, it can be a gift from You, available to all who accept. Amen.

SALVATION

Every good gift and every perfect gift is from above,
and cometh down from the father of lights.

James 1:17

God, according to Your Word, the story of salvation doesn't begin with the birth of Jesus; there has been need for a Savior since sin entered the world and Adam was banished from Eden.

Jesus was Your unfathomable, good, and perfect Christmas present to the whole world. Wrapped and swaddled, He was the "at last" gift that made salvation available to everyone, without ritual or ceremony. Centuries later, theologians would call Jesus' birth and death the means of salvation by grace, and not works.

Father, it's so appropriate for You to be declared the Father of Lights, because in Jesus, there is no darkness at all. Hallelujah! Amen.

SALVATION

The time is fulfilled, and the kingdom of God is at hand:
repent ye, and believe the gospel.

MARK 1:15

*L*ord, there will probably be a lot of serious repenting going on in many homes the day after Christmas. Spending limits will have been transgressed, as well as diets and other will power-related practices.

And as if folks didn't learn their lessons on Black Friday, the Day-After Half-Off Sales will lure plastic back out of our wallets just one more time.

It is the lure of the world that necessitates Your provision for repentance, a primary step in salvation. It's remarkable how easy it was to ask forgiveness as children, and now as so-called sophisticated adults, it's often more important to save face.

Father God, allow me to regain some of those child-like qualities that allowed me to freely kneel or write or even shed a tear or two in repentance for sin, intentional or otherwise. Amen.

SALVATION

My grace is sufficient for thee:
for my strength is made perfect in weakness.
2 CORINTHIANS 12:9

*H*eavenly Father, the classic meaning of divine grace is the offering of undeserved and unmerited love and favor from You. It's Your saving activity on my behalf. You love me so much that You provide me salvation (forgiveness and eternal life), through Your Son, Jesus. That's grace. That's what is so remarkable about You, Father.

Acts says that Stephen, the first Christian martyr, was "full of grace and God's Holy Spirit" (Acts 6:8; 7:55). That type of grace is a quality in my life that shouts Your presence, even when I don't open my mouth.

Lord, as I rub shoulders with friends, relatives, and total strangers over Christmas, grant that the quality of my life will reflect Jesus. Amen.

SALVATION

Let the words of my mouth, and the meditation
of my heart, be acceptable in thy sight, O LORD,
my strength, and my redeemer.

PSALM 19:14

*F*ather, as I anticipate the good things that Christmas has in store, what is it I still want and need? The tree is up and decorated, the crèche is unwrapped and in place, the outdoor lights are strung, and there just may be an evergreen wreath on the door. Now what?

While it would be nice to start the Christmas cookies and to finish any last-minute handmade presents, Lord, I pray that my words and thoughts this Christmas will be pleasing to You. Help me uphold my responsibility of praise, because You gave me Jesus, and I want everyone to know Him. Amen.